Vocabulary Workshop
New Edition

Level Blue

Jerome Shostak

Consultants

Virginia M. Russell
Director of Clinical Experiences
Hunter College, School of Education
New York, NY

Elaine M. Czarnecki
Literacy Consultant
Annapolis, MD

Diane Flora
Reading Specialist
Indianapolis, IN

Sadlier-Oxford
A Division of William H. Sadlier, Inc.

Vocabulary Workshop
New Edition

Reviewers
The publisher wishes to thank the following teachers for their thorough review and thoughtful comments on portions of the series prior to publication.

Sharon West
Fifth Grade Teacher
Tallahassee, FL

Patty Bowman
Fifth Grade Teacher
Plano, TX

Debbie Dantin
Fifth Grade Teacher
Marrero, LA

Photo Credits
Christie's Images Ltd: 13.
Corbis/Bettmann: 51, 63, 142; Michael Busselle: 57; Hulton-Deutsch Collection: 103.

Everett Collection: 19.

Getty Images/Hulton Archive: 25, 70; Stone/Lorne Resnick: 45; Photodisc: 83; Stone/Lornetz Gullachsen: 85; Stone/Bruce Forster: 97; National Geographic/Walter Meayers Edwards: 110; Stone/Michael Rosenfeld: 117; Stone/Gary Holscher: 135; Reportage/Ezra Shaw: 155.

The Granger Collection: *New York*: 38.

PunchStock/Panoramic Images: 129.

retrofile.com/C.P. Cushing: 91.

robertstock.com: 31.

Illustrator
Daryl Stevens: 43, 75, 115, 147.

Printed in the United States of America.
ISBN: 978-0-8215-0365-2
21 22 23 25 25 BRR 16 15 14 13

CONTENTS

Foreword 4

The Vocabulary of Vocabulary 5

Pronunciation Key 9

Diagnostic Test 10

Unit One 12

Unit Two 18

Unit Three 24

Unit Four 30

   Review (Units One–Four) 36

Unit Five 44

Unit Six 50

Unit Seven 56

Unit Eight 62

   Review (Units Five–Eight) 68

   Cumulative Review I (Units One–Eight) 76

Unit Nine 84

Unit Ten 90

Unit Eleven 96

Unit Twelve 102

   Review (Units Nine–Twelve) 108

Unit Thirteen 116

Unit Fourteen 122

Unit Fifteen 128

Unit Sixteen 134

   Review (Units Thirteen–Sixteen) 140

   Cumulative Review II (Units Nine–Sixteen) 148

Final Mastery Test 156

Index 160

FOREWORD

For over half a century Vocabulary Workshop has proven a highly successful tool for promoting and guiding systematic vocabulary growth. Level Blue is meant both to help younger students *increase* their vocabulary and to *improve* their vocabulary skills. It has also been designed to help prepare students for vocabulary-related items found in standardized tests.

This New Edition of Vocabulary Workshop Level Blue maintains the core of the original edition—the Word List and the 16 Units—and introduces in the restructured Reviews and Cumulative Reviews several important new features:

- **Vocabulary for Comprehension** is modeled on the reading sections of standardized tests, and, as in those tests, presents reading comprehension questions, including vocabulary-related ones, based on a reading passage. Representing a variety of genres—both fiction and nonfiction—these reading passages offer students practice with many types of text.

- **Grammar in Context** is linked to the Vocabulary for Comprehension passage, referring to a grammar, usage, or mechanics skill illustrated in that passage. Grammar in Context is designed to give students instruction and practice in the grammar skills commonly assessed on standardized tests and, at the same time, to improve their writing by giving students a stronger footing in the conventions of standard English.

- **Completing the Idea** gives students a prompt, in the form of a sentence-starter that contains a taught word, and invites them to complete a thought in any way that they like. This exercise offers students the opportunity to express themselves, and teachers a way of assessing how well their students have mastered the meaning and usage of the taught words.

- **Write Your Own** provides students an opportunity to write an original sentence that correctly uses one of the taught words and that illustrates the grammar skill discussed in the foregoing Grammar in Context exercise.

- **Building with Latin and Greek Roots** shows students how the knowledge of a word stemming from a Latin or Greek root can help them uncover the meaning of other words containing that same root.

Also new to this edition are **Interactive Online Activities** that extend and enrich the instruction and practice contained in the student text. These online activities cover all 192 taught words with engaging word games and crossword puzzles. Access to these free activities is available at www.sadlier-oxford.com.

THE VOCABULARY OF VOCABULARY

English has a large group of special terms to describe how words are used and how they are related to one another. These terms make up what we might call the "vocabulary of vocabulary." Learning to understand and use the vocabulary of vocabulary will help you to get better results in your vocabulary-building program.

Part of Speech

Every word in English plays some role in the language. What that role is determines how a word is classified grammatically. These classifications are called "parts of speech." In English there are eight parts of speech: nouns, pronouns, verbs, adjectives, adverbs, prepositions, conjunctions, and interjections. All of the words introduced in this book are nouns (abbreviated *n.*), verbs (*v.*), or adjectives (*adj.*).

A **noun** names a person, place, or thing. *Uncle, home,* and *food* are nouns. So are *Lincoln, Chicago,* and *Superbowl.* Nouns also name things such as ideas and feelings; for example, *justice, space,* and *anger* are nouns.

Verbs express action or a state of being. *Go, be, live, tell, write, speak, listen, leave, arrive,* and *behave* are verbs.

Adjectives describe or give information about nouns or other adjectives. *Happy, sad, quick, slow, big, little, black, white, first,* and *last* are adjectives.

Many English words act as more than one part of speech. The word *bend,* for example, can be a verb or a noun. Its part of speech depends upon the way it is used.

NOUN: We came to a bend in the river. [*bend* names a thing]

VERB: The wind made the trees bend. [*bend* expresses an action]

EXERCISES   For each sentence, circle the choice that identifies the part of speech of the word in **boldface**.

1. My brother is a **fast** runner.

    a. noun   b. verb   c. adjective

2. Let's **work** together to solve the problem.

    a. noun   b. verb   c. adjective

3. I have a lot of **work** to do this weekend.

    a. noun   b. verb   c. adjective

4. I'm wearing a **new** pair of socks.

    a. noun   b. verb   c. adjective

5. There were a lot of happy **faces** in the crowd.

    a. noun   b. verb   c. adjective

6. The front of the house **faces** East.

    a. noun   b. verb   c. adjective

Synonyms and Antonyms

Synonyms

A **synonym** is a word that means *the same* or *nearly the same* as another word.

EXAMPLES   gift — present   smart — clever

cry — weep   joy — happiness

thin — skinny   begin — start

EXERCISES   For each of the following groups, circle the choice that is most nearly the **same** in meaning as the word in **boldface**.

1. **silent**	2. **jog**	3. **law**	4. **tidy**
a. noisy	a. crawl	a. rule	a. messy
b. kind	b. trot	b. school	b. small
c. playful	c. laugh	c. jail	c. new
d. quiet	d. stop	d. sheriff	d. neat

Antonyms

An **antonym** is a word that is *opposite* or *nearly opposite* in meaning to another word.

EXAMPLES   grow — shrink   huge — tiny

crowded — empty   victory — defeat

friend — enemy   hide — show

EXERCISES   For each of the following groups, circle the choice that is most nearly **opposite** in meaning to the word in **boldface**.

1. **simple**	2. **wealth**	3. **punish**	4. **healthy**
a. easy	a. fame	a. reward	a. bossy
b. difficult	b. success	b. trust	b. messy
c. cheap	c. poverty	c. trick	c. sturdy
d. boring	d. taxes	d. remember	d. sickly

Context Clues

When you turn to the "Completing the Sentence" and "Vocabulary for Comprehension" exercises in this book, look for clues built into the passages to guide you to the correct answers. There are three basic types of clues.

Restatement Clues A restatement clue gives a *definition of*, or a *synonym for*, a missing word.

EXAMPLE The climbers slowly made their way to the <u>top of the mountain</u> until at last they reached its very _____.

a. bottom   b. slope   (c.) peak   d. range

Contrast Clues A contrast clue gives an *antonym for*, or a phrase meaning *the opposite of*, a missing word.

EXAMPLE The weather was <u>mild</u> at the foot of the mountain, but the conditions at the top were _____.

a. nice   (b.) harsh   c. friendly   d. dry

Situational Clues Sometimes the situation itself, as it is outlined in the sentence or passage, suggests the word that is missing but does not state the meaning directly.

EXAMPLE After the <u>long and dangerous</u> return from the top of the mountain, the climbers were very _____.

a. bored   (b.) weary   c. fresh   d. guilty

To figure out which word is missing from the sentence, ask yourself this question: How would the climbers feel after a "long and dangerous" journey? Would they feel bored? Weary? Fresh? Guilty?

EXERCISES Use context clues to choose the word that best completes each of the following sentences.

1. Why argue over such silly matters when we have so many _____ problems to deal with?

   a. little   b. foolish   c. serious   d. unimportant

2. We will have to _____ for hours to get rid of all the grime.

   a. play   b. read   c. sing   d. scrub

3. The noise in the crowded gym was so great that we could barely make ourselves heard above the _____.

   a. racket   b. score   c. chairs   d. clock

Analogies

An **analogy** is a comparison. For example, we can make an analogy, or comparison, between a computer and a human brain.

In this book, you will be asked to find the relationship between two words. Then, to show that you understand that relationship, you will be asked to choose another pair of words that shows the same relationship.

EXAMPLES

1. **close** is to **open** as

   a. dance is to swim

   b. hold is to pinch

   c. stop is to go

   d. talk is to chat

2. **push** is to **shove** as

   a. grab is to release

   b. giggle is to laugh

   c. hope is to try

   d. watch is to listen

In the first example, note that *close* and *open* are **antonyms**; they are opposite in meaning. Of the four choices given, which pair is made up of words that are also antonyms, or opposite in meaning? The answer, of course, is *c, stop is to go*.

In the second example, note that *push* and *shove* are **synonyms**; they have nearly the same meaning. Of the four choices given, which pair is made up of words that are also synonyms, or nearly the same in meaning? The answer is *b, giggle is to laugh*.

There are many other kinds of analogies besides ones based on synonyms and antonyms. For each of the exercises that follow, first study carefully the pair of words in **boldface**. Then, when you have figured out the relationship between the two words, look for another pair that has the same relationship. Circle the item that best completes the analogy, and then write the relationship on the lines provided.

3. **steel** is to **metal** as

   a. oak is to wood

   b. pencil is to pen

   c. glass is to bottle

   d. jewel is to diamond

4. **petal** is to **flower** as

   a. baseball is to hockey

   b. cover is to magazine

   c. letter is to note

   d. branch is to tree

5. **kitten** is to **cat** as

   a. chick is to egg

   b. horse is to colt

   c. puppy is to dog

   d. cub is to den

Relationship: _____

_____

_____

_____

Relationship: _____

_____

_____

_____

Relationship: _____

_____

_____

_____

PRONUNCIATION KEY

The pronunciation is given for every basic word introduced in this book. The symbols, which are shown below, are similar to those that appear in most standard dictionaries. The author has consulted a large number of dictionaries for this purpose but has relied primarily on *Webster's Third New International Dictionary* and *The Random House Dictionary of the English Language (Unabridged)*.

Of course, there are many English words, including some that appear in this book, for which two (or more) pronunciations are commonly accepted. In virtually all cases where such words occur in this book, just one pronunciation is given. Exceptions to this rule are made, however, in cases when the pronunciation of a word changes according to its part of speech. For example, as a noun the word *object* is pronounced **äb′ jekt**; as a verb it is pronounced **əb jekt′**. These relatively simple pronunciation guides should be readily usable by students. It should be emphasized, however, that the best way to learn the pronunciation of a word is to listen to and imitate an educated speaker.

Vowels	ā	l*a*ke	e	str*e*ss	u	r*u*g
	a	m*a*t	ī	kn*i*fe	ü	b*oo*t, n*ew*
	â	c*a*re	i	s*i*t	u̇	f*oo*t, p*u*ll
	ä	b*a*rk, b*o*ttle	ō	fl*o*w	ə	*a*go, brok*e*n
	au̇	d*ou*bt	ô	*a*ll, c*o*rd	ûr	h*er*d, b*ir*d,
	ē	b*ea*t, word*y*	oi	*oi*l		p*ur*se

Consonants	ch	*ch*ild, lecture	s	*c*ellar	wh	*wh*at
	g	*g*ive	sh	*sh*un	y	*y*ell
	j	*g*entle, bri*dge*	th	*th*ank	z	i*s*
	ŋ	si*ng*	t̶h̶	*th*ose	zh	mea*s*ure

All other consonants are sounded as in the alphabet.

Stress	The accent mark *follows* the syllable receiving the major stress: en rich′.

9

For each of the following items, circle the letter for the word or phrase that best expresses the meaning of the word in **boldface** in the introductory phrase.

Example

a **frisky** puppy

a. wet   (b.) playful   c. sick   d. little

---

1. a **fragile** set of crystal glasses
   a. shiny   b. beautiful   c. matched   d. delicate

2. read about the **dispute**
   a. agreement   b. argument   c. election   d. discovery

3. **bluffed** a throw to first base
   a. caught   b. dropped   c. blocked   d. faked

4. painted in **vivid** colors
   a. brilliant   b. matching   c. contrasting   d. dull

5. a **span** of ninety feet
   a. ditch   b. length   c. road   d. depth

6. **lingered** at a party
   a. left   b. entertained   c. danced   d. stayed

7. lived like **nomads**
   a. athletes   b. wanderers   c. criminals   d. farmers

8. a **festive** mood
   a. sad   b. angry   c. generous   d. happy

9. a **keen** mind
   a. silly   b. troubled   c. sharp   d. dull

10. **composed** beautiful songs
    a. sang   b. wrote   c. played   d. listened to

11. a very **reliable** mechanic
    a. trustworthy   b. skilled   c. talkative   d. cheerful

12. wrote about her **feats**
    a. poems   b. relatives   c. deeds   d. shoes

13. the **primary** reason
    a. only   b. main   c. secret   d. wrong

14. **cherish** your friends
    a. argue with   b. forget   c. visit   d. treasure

15. made an **improper** turn
    a. wrong   b. left   c. unnecessary   d. sudden

16. survived a **famine**
    a. lack of shelter   b. lack of food   c. lack of news   d. lack of taste

17. **appealed** for volunteers
    a. voted   b. telephoned   c. asked   d. paid

18. an important **principle**
    a. act   b. goal   c. teacher   d. rule

19. a totally **absurd** idea
    a. interesting   b. foolish   c. sensible   d. confusing

20. **shreds** of paper
    a. bits   b. piles   c. pads   d. boxes

21. a **pitiless** dictator
    a. friendless   b. powerful   c. cheerful   d. heartless

22. surrounded by many **foes**
    a. deer   b. friends   c. enemies   d. neighbors

23. **pursued** the runaway horse
    a. chased   b. rode   c. saddled   d. fed

24. a **universal** problem
    a. worldwide   b. local   c. recent   d. temporary

25. enjoyed special holiday **fare**
    a. prayers   b. games   c. music   d. food and drink

Definitions

Study the spelling, pronunciation, part of speech, and definition given for each of the words below. Write the word in the blank space in the sentence that follows. Then read the synonyms and antonyms.

1. **blunder**
   (blun' dər)

   (v.) to make a foolish or careless mistake; to move clumsily and carelessly
   I saw the hiker _____ through the woods.
   (n.) a serious or thoughtless mistake
   I was terribly embarrassed by my _____.
   SYNONYMS: (v.) to err, foul up, bungle, goof; (n.) an error, blooper
   ANTONYMS: (v.) to triumph, succeed; (n.) a success, hit

2. **cancel**
   (kan' səl)

   (v.) to call off or do away with; to cross out with lines or other marks to show that something cannot be used again
   Maybe the principal will _____ classes if it continues to snow.
   SYNONYMS: to stop, discontinue, drop, repeal, revoke
   ANTONYMS: to renew, continue, extend, maintain

3. **continuous**
   (kən tin' yü əs)

   (adj.) going on without a stop or break
   _____ TV coverage began shortly after news of the disaster broke.
   SYNONYMS: ongoing, endless, ceaseless, unbroken, constant, perpetual
   ANTONYMS: broken, discontinuous, interrupted

4. **distribute**
   (di stri' byüt)

   (v.) to give out in shares; to scatter or spread
   Our class will _____ leaflets announcing the school's fund-raising drive.
   SYNONYMS: to divide, share, deal, issue
   ANTONYMS: to gather, collect, hold

5. **document**
   (dä' kyə ment)

   (n.) a written or printed record that gives information or proof
   The librarian found the old _____ between the pages of a book.
   (v.) to give written or printed proof; to support with evidence
   Writers often _____ their sources.
   SYNONYMS: (n.) a certificate, deed; (v.) to prove, establish

6. **fragile**
   (fra' jəl)

   (adj.) easily broken or damaged, requiring special handling or care
   The _____ antique was carefully packed to protect it during shipment.
   SYNONYMS: weak, frail, breakable, delicate, brittle, flimsy
   ANTONYMS: sturdy, hardy, strong, rugged, tough

Internet

For vocabulary games and activities, visit **www.sadlier-oxford.com**.

The Greek god Zeus, shown here in a Roman sculpture, is the subject of many ancient **myths** (word 7).

7. **myth**
   (miŧh)

(n.) an old story that explains why something is or how it came to be; something imaginary

The play is based on an ancient Greek _____.

SYNONYMS: a legend, fable, tale, fantasy, fairy tale
ANTONYM: a fact

8. **reject**
   (ri jekt')

(v.) to refuse to accept, agree to, believe, or use

Why did you _____ the offer?

SYNONYMS: to deny, discard, junk, scrap, decline, dismiss
ANTONYMS: to take, accept, receive, welcome

9. **scuffle**
   (sku' fəl)

(v.) to fight or struggle closely with

A witness saw the two men _____ in an alley.

(n.) fight or struggle

Police officers were called in to break up the _____.

SYNONYMS: (v.) to tussle, roughhouse, battle, brawl; (n.) a fistfight, clash

10. **solitary**
    (sä' lə ter ē)

(adj.) living or being alone; being the only one

The old man led a _____ life.

SYNONYMS: single, sole, lone
ANTONYMS: sociable; several, many, numerous

11. **temporary**
    (tem' pə rer ē)

(adj.) lasting or used for a limited time

A blow to the head can cause a _____ loss of memory.

SYNONYMS: short-term, passing, brief, momentary
ANTONYMS: lasting, long-lived, permanent

12. **veteran**
    (ve' tə rən)

(n.) a person who has served in the armed forces; a person who has a lot of experience

The President spoke to a group of combat _____.

(adj.) having much experience in some job or field, seasoned

In her next movie, the actress will play a _____ reporter.

SYNONYMS: (adj.) expert, professional, experienced, skilled, accomplished
ANTONYMS: (n.) a beginner, newcomer, novice, rookie

13

For each item below, choose the word whose meaning is suggested by the clue given. Then write the word in the space provided.

1. A roommate you have for only a month is a _____ one.
   a. continuous   b. temporary   c. fragile   d. solitary

2. A black eye might be the result of a _____.
   a. scuffle   b. myth   c. veteran   d. blunder

3. To _____ your age you might show a birth certificate or a driver's license.
   a. distribute   b. document   c. cancel   d. reject

4. A person who lives alone in the woods might be described as _____.
   a. continuous   b. solitary   c. temporary   d. fragile

5. The idea that you will get warts from touching a frog is a _____.
   a. blunder   b. document   c. scuffle   d. myth

6. If I make a serious mistake, I commit a _____.
   a. scuffle   b. document   c. myth   d. blunder

7. A box containing an item that can be broken easily might be stamped "_____."
   a. solitary   b. temporary   c. fragile   d. continuous

8. A charity might _____ food to the homeless.
   a. reject   b. cancel   c. scuffle   d. distribute

9. Something that goes on without stopping is _____.
   a. continuous   b. temporary   c. solitary   d. fragile

10. To refuse a gift is to _____ it.
    a. cancel   b. scuffle   c. distribute   d. reject

11. A person who has a lot of experience at something is a _____.
    a. blunder   b. myth   c. document   d. veteran

12. If I call off a party, I _____ it.
    a. reject   b. blunder   c. cancel   d. scuffle

Synonyms

*For each item below, choose the word that is most nearly the **same** in meaning as the word or phrase in **boldface.** Then write your choice on the line provided.*

1. a **constant** flow of traffic
   a. fragile   b. temporary   c. continuous   d. veteran   _____

2. tried to hide the **blooper**
   a. document   b. myth   c. blunder   d. scuffle   _____

3. not a **single** cent
   a. temporary   b. fragile   c. solitary   d. veteran   _____

4. witnessed the **fight**
   a. myth   b. blunder   c. document   d. scuffle   _____

5. very important **records**
   a. veterans   b. documents   c. myths   d. blunders   _____

6. a collection of ancient **stories**
   a. documents   b. myths   c. veterans   d. blunders   _____

Antonyms

*For each item below, choose the word that is most nearly **opposite** in meaning to the word or phrase in **boldface.** Then write your choice on the line provided.*

1. **renew** my subscription
   a. cancel   b. blunder   c. scuffle   d. distribute   _____

2. **accept** the marriage proposal
   a. scuffle   b. reject   c. blunder   d. distribute   _____

3. a **novice** mountain climber
   a. temporary   b. fragile   c. continuous   d. veteran   _____

4. **collect** the homework sheets
   a. reject   b. document   c. distribute   d. cancel   _____

5. a **sturdy** device
   a. temporary   b. solitary   c. veteran   d. fragile   _____

6. a **permanent** filling
   a. veteran   b. continuous   c. temporary   d. solitary   _____

From the list of words on pages 12–13, choose the one that best completes each item below. Then write the word in the space provided. (You may have to change the word's ending.)

A VISIT TO A MUSEUM

■ Our class visited the museum on the last day of a(n) _____ exhibit of ancient Greek vases. The vases had been on display for three months and were going to be returned to the European museums that had lent them.

■ Some of the vases were more than 2,000 years old. Because they were so old and _____, we weren't allowed to touch them.

■ Security guards kept visitors a few feet from the display cases, so there was no chance that someone could _____ into them.

■ The guide told us that the pictures painted on some of the vases were not of real people but characters from legends and _____.

■ One picture showed a(n) _____ warrior fighting off a band of attackers. Our guide explained that the lone fighter was the Greek warrior Achilles and that his attackers were soldiers of Troy.

A FAMOUS DECLARATION

■ In refusing to accept English rule, the writers of the Declaration of Independence _____ the claim that Parliament had sovereignty, or lawful power, over the American colonies.

■ Those who supported the cause of American independence quickly printed and _____ copies of the Declaration throughout the thirteen colonies.

■ The original _____, one of America's historic treasures, is now on view at the National Archives building in Washington, D.C.

ON THE SOCCER FIELD

■ Two days of _____ rain had turned the soccer field into a sea of mud and threatened to spoil the opening game of the season.

■ Before the game began, a _____ broke out in the stands when a few home-team fans came to blows with those rooting for the visiting team.

■ The referee threatened to _____ the game and send all of the fans home if order was not restored.

■ Only when a handful of popular _____ from both teams asked the fans to behave themselves did they finally settle down and let the game get under way.

Word Associations

*Circle the letter next to the word or expression that best completes the sentence or answers the question. Pay special attention to the word in **boldface**.*

1. A person might emerge from a **scuffle**
   a. with spaghetti and meatballs
   b. with scrapes and bruises
   c. with dollars and cents
   d. with hugs and kisses

2. Someone who has **blundered** would
   a. feel embarrassed
   b. be confident
   c. feel proud
   d. be rewarded

3. A **solitary** tree would probably
   a. have needles
   b. be chopped down
   c. change color in the fall
   d. stand alone

4. A **continuous** loud noise might
   a. be hard to hear
   b. stop and start
   c. be soothing
   d. be annoying

5. Which of the following is a **document**?
   a. an old friend
   b. a telephone call
   c. a marriage license
   d. a good meal

6. If I **cancel** my piano lesson,
   a. I don't go
   b. I play very well
   c. I repair the piano
   d. I arrive late

7. A **temporary** problem is one that
   a. lasts a long time
   b. goes away
   c. no one can solve
   d. anyone can solve

8. In a **veteran's** closet you might find
   a. a skateboard
   b. a party dress
   c. a box of marbles
   d. an old uniform

9. When a teacher **distributes** a test
   a. he or she grades it
   b. he or she loses it
   c. he or she passes it out
   d. he or she collects it

10. Which of the following is usually **fragile**?
    a. a hammer
    b. a pair of scissors
    c. a lightbulb
    d. a padlock

11. Someone who has been **rejected**
    a. might feel hurt
    b. might feel happy
    c. might get lost
    d. might get a cold

12. Which is a creature of **myth**?
    a. a rabbit
    b. a giraffe
    c. a duck
    d. a dragon

Definitions

Study the spelling, pronunciation, part of speech, and definition given for each of the words below. Write the word in the blank space in the sentence that follows. Then read the synonyms and antonyms.

1. **abandon**
(ə ban′ dən)

(v.) to give up on completely; to leave with no intention of returning
The captain gave the order to _____ ship.

SYNONYMS: to desert, forsake, cease, surrender
ANTONYMS: to continue, stay, remain, occupy

2. **assault**
(ə sôlt′)

(n.) a violent attack
The victim was seriously injured in the _____.

(v.) to attack violently or suddenly
Dad dared us to _____ his snow fort.

SYNONYMS: (n.) an invasion, raid, mugging, beating; (v.) to besiege, storm
ANTONYMS: (v.) to protect, defend, resist

3. **convert**
(v., kən vûrt′;
n., kän′ vûrt)

(v.) to change from one form to another
A drop in temperature to 32° F will _____ water to ice.

(n.) a person who has changed from one opinion, belief, or religion to another
The new _____ was introduced to the congregation.

SYNONYMS: (v.) to transform, turn, alter, switch
ANTONYMS: (v.) to maintain, conserve, remain

4. **dispute**
(di spyüt′)

(v.) to argue, debate, quarrel over; to question or doubt the truth of
The committee members did not _____ the merits of the bill.

(n.) an argument, quarrel, debate
Why not try to resolve the _____ peacefully?

SYNONYMS: (v.) to differ, disagree; contest, challenge; (n.) a conflict, disagreement, controversy
ANTONYMS: (v.) to agree, harmonize; (n.) an agreement, understanding, accord

5. **impressive**
(im pre′ siv)

(adj.) having a strong effect, commanding attention
The skater gave an _____ performance.

SYNONYMS: memorable, striking, stirring, thrilling, awesome, splendid
ANTONYMS: inferior, mediocre

6. **justify**
(jus′ tə fī)

(v.) to show to be fair or right; to give good reasons for
Be prepared to _____ your behavior.

SYNONYMS: to defend, explain, support, excuse
ANTONYMS: to convict, blame, accuse

For vocabulary games and activities, visit **www.sadlier-oxford.com**.

In old movies the **villain** (word 12) often wore a black hat.

7. **misleading**
(mis lē' diŋ)

(adj.) tending to give a wrong idea, often on purpose
The lawyer called the statement _____.

SYNONYMS: deceptive, false, tricky, inaccurate
ANTONYMS: direct, honest, true, accurate, straightforward

8. **numerous**
(nüm' rəs)

(adj.) many or very many
_____ *aunts and uncles came to our family reunion.*

SYNONYMS: several, plenty, plentiful
ANTONYM: few

9. **productive**
(prə duk' tiv)

(adj.) making or capable of making large amounts of; giving good results
With care it may become a _____ *orchard.*

SYNONYMS: energetic, effective, fruitful, efficient, worthwhile
ANTONYMS: unproductive, idle, useless, inactive

10. **shrewd**
(shrüd)

(adj.) showing clever judgment and practical understanding
My aunt is a _____ *businesswoman.*

SYNONYMS: artful, wise, sharp, crafty, wily, cunning
ANTONYMS: slow, stupid, dull-witted

11. **strategy**
(stra' tə jē)

(n.) a carefully made plan or plot; a plan of military operations
Our teacher suggested a test-taking _____.

SYNONYMS: an approach, design, method, scheme

12. **villain**
(vi' lən)

(n.) an evil or wicked person or character, especially in a story or play
I am going to play the _____ *in the show.*

SYNONYMS: a scoundrel, rascal, outlaw, criminal
ANTONYMS: a hero, heroine, champion

Match the Meaning

For each item below, choose the word whose meaning is suggested by the clue given. Then write the word in the space provided.

1. A violent or sudden attack is called a(n) _____.
   a. convert   b. assault   c. strategy   d. villain

2. When I carefully make a plan, I am preparing my _____.
   a. convert   b. dispute   c. villain   d. strategy

3. People who change their religion are _____ to the new religion.
   a. disputes   b. converts   c. strategies   d. villains

4. To give reasons for what you do is to _____ your actions.
   a. justify   b. abandon   c. assault   d. convert

5. Some advertisements can be _____ if they leave out key details or make false claims.
   a. misleading   b. numerous   c. productive   d. impressive

6. The most wicked character in the story is the _____.
   a. assault   b. dispute   c. villain   d. strategy

7. A vegetarian cookbook might give _____ recipes for rice dishes and fruit salads.
   a. productive   b. shrewd   c. misleading   d. numerous

8. To give up on something is to _____ it.
   a. assault   b. abandon   c. convert   d. justify

9. Another word for an argument or quarrel is a _____.
   a. convert   b. strategy   c. villain   d. dispute

10. A(n) _____ person is one who gets a lot done.
    a. productive   b. shrewd   c. misleading   d. impressive

11. The Grand Canyon is a(n) _____ sight.
    a. shrewd   b. misleading   c. impressive   d. numerous

12. To be clever and practical is to be _____.
    a. misleading   b. shrewd   c. productive   d. numerous

Synonyms

*For each item below, choose the word that is most nearly the **same** in meaning as the word or phrase in **boldface.** Then write your choice on the line provided.*

1. **change** starch to sugar
   a. abandon   b. assault   c. dispute   d. convert   _____

2. **supported** the decision
   a. abandoned   b. assaulted   c. justified   d. converted   _____

3. a **thrilling** performance
   a. misleading   b. numerous   c. shrewd   d. impressive   _____

4. tried to be more **effective**
   a. numerous   b. misleading   c. productive   d. shrewd   _____

5. a problem-solving **approach**
   a. strategy   b. assault   c. dispute   d. villain   _____

6. a **crafty** move
   a. misleading   b. impressive   c. shrewd   d. productive   _____

Antonyms

*For each item below, choose the word that is most nearly **opposite** in meaning to the word or phrase in **boldface.** Then write your choice on the line provided.*

1. **agreed with** the umpire's call
   a. disputed   b. assaulted   c. converted   d. justified   _____

2. **few** paint colors
   a. shrewd   b. misleading   c. numerous   d. productive   _____

3. **occupy** the old shack
   a. assault   b. convert   c. abandon   d. justify   _____

4. **defended** the bridge
   a. converted   b. assaulted   c. disputed   d. justified   _____

5. the **hero** of the movie
   a. convert   b. assault   c. strategy   d. villain   _____

6. gave **accurate** directions to the tourist
   a. impressive   b. misleading   c. numerous   d. productive   _____

Completing the Sentence

From the list of words on pages 18–19, choose the one that best completes each item below. Then write the word in the space provided. (You may have to change the word's ending.)

GREEKS AND TROJANS AT WAR

■ Both the Greek poet Homer and the Roman poet Virgil wrote of the ten-year siege of Troy by the Greeks and of the heroes and _____ who did battle there.

■ One of the most famous stories describes the sly _____ that the Greeks thought up to defeat the Trojans.

■ The Greeks had tried not once but on _____ occasions to force the Trojans to surrender the fortress city.

■ Several times the Greeks had _____ the walls of Troy, but all of the attacks had failed.

■ Finally, the Greeks came up with a _____ plan: They left at the gates of Troy a huge wooden horse as a pretended peace offering. The Trojans brought the horse inside the city walls.

■ But the wooden horse was a _____ gift, for hidden inside its huge body was a small army of Greeks, who at nightfall climbed from the horse and opened the gates to the city.

A FALSE SCIENCE

■ Alchemists were people who believed that it was possible to _____ ordinary metals, such as iron and lead, into gold. The best-known alchemists are those who practiced in Europe during the Middle Ages.

■ They staged very _____ experiments to try to convince others that they could do as they promised.

■ Some people believed that the possibility of great wealth _____ even the most far-fetched experiments.

■ Scientists today would _____ the ideas of the alchemists, but centuries ago many people believed that their ideas were sound. In fact, it was not until the 1800s that scientists proved that base metals cannot be turned into gold.

■ Failure upon failure finally persuaded most alchemists to _____ their dreams of wealth and glory.

■ In a way, the work that the alchemists did was _____ because it sometimes led to advances in chemistry. During the Middle Ages, for example, alchemists were responsible for the discovery of mineral acids.

Word Associations

*Circle the letter next to the word or expression that best completes the sentence or answers the question. Pay special attention to the word in **boldface**.*

1. A person who has been **abandoned**
   a. would feel powerful
   b. would feel bold
   c. would feel happy
   d. would feel lonely

2. If you **convert** a room, you
   a. leave it the same
   b. hide in it
   c. change it
   d. take a picture of it

3. You might expect a **villain** to
   a. volunteer in a soup kitchen
   b. receive an award
   c. play the cello
   d. kidnap someone

4. A really **impressive** baseball team would
   a. use extra players
   b. lack the proper equipment
   c. lead the league
   d. play only night games

5. Which might stop an **assault**?
   a. a good night's sleep
   b. a police officer
   c. a salt shaker
   d. a rocking horse

6. A winning **strategy** involves
   a. careful planning
   b. lots of money
   c. powerful friends
   d. reckless bravery

7. On a **productive** day you would
   a. play outside
   b. get a lot done
   c. stay inside
   d. get nothing done

8. If your friends are **numerous**
   a. you have very few of them
   b. they live nearby
   c. you have a lot of them
   d. they live far away

9. **Misleading** information should usually be
   a. ignored
   b. memorized
   c. published
   d. relied upon

10. When I **justify** my claims
    a. I take them back
    b. I lose them
    c. I defend them
    d. I get sued

11. A **shrewd** person would probably
    a. get lost
    b. get a good deal
    c. get a warm welcome
    d. get fooled

12. The best way to end a **dispute** is to
    a. shake hands
    b. skip lunch
    c. argue
    d. wrestle

Unit 2 ■ 23

Definitions

Study the spelling, pronunciation, part of speech, and definition given for each of the words below. Write the word in the blank space in the sentence that follows. Then read the synonyms and antonyms.

1. **bluff**
   (bluf)

   (adj.) direct and outspoken in a good-natured way
   He seemed a hearty, _____ fellow.
   (n.) a steep, high cliff or bank; an attempt to fool someone
   A scout stood on a _____ overlooking the valley.
   (v.) to deceive or trick; to try to fool others by putting on a confident front
   The thieves tried to _____ their way past the security guard.

   SYNONYMS: (adj.) hearty; (n.) a ridge; a trick, hoax; (v.) to mislead, pretend, fake
   ANTONYMS: (adj.) insincere, artful, sly

2. **cautious**
   (kô′ shəs)

   (adj.) avoiding unnecessary risks or mistakes
   A _____ traveler prepares for emergencies.

   SYNONYMS: careful, watchful, wary, guarded
   ANTONYMS: daring, reckless, wild

3. **consist**
   (kən sist′)

   (v.) (used with *of*) to be made up of
   Many salad dressings _____ of oil, vinegar, and spices.

   SYNONYMS: to contain, include, involve, comprise

4. **despise**
   (di spīz′)

   (v.) to look down on intensely or feel contempt for, dislike strongly
   I _____ bullies.

   SYNONYMS: to hate, scorn, detest, loathe
   ANTONYMS: to love, admire, esteem, adore, praise

5. **haven**
   (hā′ vən)

   (n.) a safe place
   The captain sought a _____ from the storm.

   SYNONYMS: a harbor, port, refuge, retreat, shelter, sanctuary
   ANTONYMS: a trap, snare, ambush

6. **miniature**
   (mi′ nē ə chŭr)

   (n.) a very small copy, model, or painting
   Her collection of _____ is quite valuable.
   (adj.) on a very small scale
   A _____ railroad was on display in the toy department of the store.

   SYNONYMS: (adj.) little, tiny, minute
   ANTONYMS: (adj.) huge, giant

Queen Victoria was Great Britain's **monarch** (word 7) from 1837 until 1901, when she died at the age of 81.

7. **monarch**
(mä′ nərk)

(n.) a person who rules over a kingdom or empire
The archbishop crowned the new _____.

SYNONYMS: a ruler, king, queen, emperor, empress, czar, sovereign
ANTONYMS: a subject, follower, commoner

8. **obstacle**
(äb′ sti kəl)

(n.) something that gets in the way
Shyness need not be an _____ to success.

SYNONYMS: a hurdle, barrier, snag, hindrance
ANTONYMS: an aid, help, support, advantage

9. **postpone**
(pōst pōn′)

(v.) to put off until later
Coach decided to _____ the practice.

SYNONYMS: to delay, suspend, shelve, defer
ANTONYMS: to advance, move up

10. **straggle**
(stra′ gəl)

(v.) to stray off or trail behind; to spread out in a scattered fashion
Latecomers continued to _____ into the theater.

SYNONYMS: to ramble, drift, wander, roam, rove, detour

11. **treacherous**
(tre′ chə rəs)

(adj.) likely to betray; seemingly safe but actually dangerous
That hill can be a _____ climb in winter.

SYNONYMS: disloyal, untrustworthy, unreliable; chancy, deceptive, tricky, hazardous
ANTONYMS: faithful, trustworthy; safe, harmless

12. **vivid**
(vi′ vəd)

(adj.) bright and sharp, giving a clear picture; full of life
She gave a _____ description of the daring rescue.

SYNONYMS: lively, intense, brilliant, dazzling, spirited, clear
ANTONYMS: lifeless, dull, drab, hazy, foggy

Match the Meaning

For each item below, choose the word whose meaning is suggested by the clue given. Then write the word in the space provided.

1. A picture so brilliant and bold that it seems alive might be called

   _____.

   a. bluff   b. cautious   c. treacherous   d. vivid

2. A sundae _____ of ice cream and your choice of toppings.

   a. despises   b. consists   c. postpones   d. straggles

3. Something that blocks our way might be called a(n) _____.

   a. obstacle   b. bluff   c. haven   d. miniature

4. Hikers who stray from a trail or fall behind are guilty of _____.

   a. consisting   b. despising   c. straggling   d. postponing

5. To try to fool others by acting very confident is to _____.

   a. consist   b. despise   c. straggle   d. bluff

6. If you _____ doing a chore, you will just have to do it later.

   a. bluff   b. postpone   c. straggle   d. despise

7. Walking on a decaying log that bridges a stream could be _____.

   a. treacherous   b. cautious   c. miniature   d. bluff

8. To hate or to dislike something strongly is to _____ it.

   a. postpone   b. bluff   c. despise   d. consist

9. Another name for king is _____.

   a. haven   b. bluff   c. monarch   d. miniature

10. Boats seek a safe _____ where they can drop anchor for the night.

    a. bluff   b. obstacle   c. monarch   d. haven

11. A tiny copy of a full-sized object is known as a _____.

    a. bluff   b. miniature   c. haven   d. monarch

12. To avoid unnecessary risk is to act in a _____ way.

    a. cautious   b. vivid   c. miniature   d. treacherous

Synonyms

*For each item below, choose the word that is most nearly the same in meaning as the word or phrase in **boldface**. Then write your choice on the line provided.*

1. **fake** your way past the guard
   a. consist   b. despise   c. postpone   d. bluff   _____

2. **wander** from the route
   a. bluff   b. straggle   c. postpone   d. despise   _____

3. a peaceful **refuge** in the war-torn city
   a. haven   b. miniature   c. monarch   d. bluff   _____

4. a mix that **contained** flour, sugar, and baking powder
   a. bluffed   b. consisted of   c. despised   d. postponed   _____

5. a **watchful** driver
   a. miniature   b. treacherous   c. cautious   d. vivid   _____

6. a noble, wise, and generous **ruler**
   a. monarch   b. haven   c. obstacle   d. miniature   _____

Antonyms

*For each item below, choose the word that is most nearly opposite in meaning to the word or phrase in **boldface**. Then write your choice on the line provided.*

1. **adore** that kind of music
   a. consist   b. bluff   c. despise   d. straggle   _____

2. formed a **hazy** image
   a. treacherous   b. vivid   c. cautious   d. miniature   _____

3. to **move up** the ceremony one month
   a. postpone   b. bluff   c. despise   d. straggle   _____

4. a **huge** model of the castle
   a. cautious   b. treacherous   c. bluff   d. miniature   _____

5. a **faithful** servant
   a. treacherous   b. cautious   c. miniature   d. vivid   _____

6. no **advantage** to winning the election
   a. haven   b. obstacle   c. miniature   d. monarch   _____

Completing the Sentence

From the list of words on pages 24–25, choose the one that best completes each item below. Then write the word in the space provided. (You may have to change the word's ending.)

AMERICANS FIGHT FOR THEIR INDEPENDENCE

■ King George III was the English _____ when American colonists began to grow impatient with English rule.

■ Even colonists who were eager for independence were _____ at first because they did not want a war.

■ But not all colonists _____ British rule; nearly one-third of them believed they should stay loyal to the King.

■ The first fight took place between 700 British soldiers and a small army that _____ of 70 American volunteers called Minutemen. The site of the battle was Lexington, Massachusetts.

■ In 1780, the American General Benedict Arnold took part in a _____ plot that nearly cost the lives of three thousand American soldiers.

■ After overcoming many _____, the Americans defeated the British, and King George recognized the United States as an independent nation.

A VIEW FROM HIGH ABOVE

■ As we looked down from the rocky _____, we could see a small herd of wild ponies trotting in a field far below us.

■ We were so high above them that they looked like _____ horses.

■ One gray mare _____ behind the rest of the herd to protect her young foal.

A GETAWAY FOR PRESIDENTS

■ Since 1942, American presidents have used a quiet cabin retreat in Maryland as a _____ from the summer heat of Washington, D.C.

■ My Uncle David has _____ memories of the occasion when President Eisenhower renamed the retreat Camp David to honor the President's grandson.

■ A crisis might cause the President to _____ a planned visit to Camp David until the situation is under control.

 **Word Associations**

Circle the letter next to the word or expression that best completes the sentence or answers the question. Pay special attention to the word in **boldface.**

1. A **vivid** performance by an actor
   a. would bore you
   b. would anger you
   c. would entertain you
   d. would disappoint you

2. A **treacherous** classmate might
   a. reveal your secrets
   b. be good at science
   c. eat too much at lunch
   d. forget to wear a bike helmet

3. A person who overcomes **obstacles**
   a. is a fast runner
   b. enjoys swimming
   c. rarely follows through
   d. does not give up easily

4. If you **straggle** on a field trip
   a. you go home early
   b. you lead the way
   c. you learn a lot
   d. you might get lost

5. A cool **haven** on a hot afternoon might be
   a. a steam bath
   b. a desert
   c. a shady tree
   d. a wool sweater

6. Some people **bluff** when they
   a. take a stroll along a cliff
   b. have lunch
   c. watch television
   d. play a game

7. If you **despise** something
   a. you are surprised by it
   b. you absolutely hate it
   c. you don't care about it
   d. you like it very much

8. A **miniature** dog would probably
   a. be a good hunter
   b. eat you out of house and home
   c. have a nasty temper
   d. be small enough to hold

9. Of what does a pizza **consist**?
   a. crust, sauce, and cheese
   b. a good appetite
   c. Italian restaurants
   d. about a dollar a slice

10. Which might be **postponed** because of rain?
    a. swim meet
    b. gymnastics meet
    c. a baseball game
    d. a basketball game

11. A **cautious** skier would probably
    a. ski only at night
    b. stay on the beginner's slopes
    c. buy used equipment
    d. perform dangerous stunts

12. Which would a **monarch** wear?
    a. a parka
    b. a baseball hat
    c. a crown
    d. a bathing suit

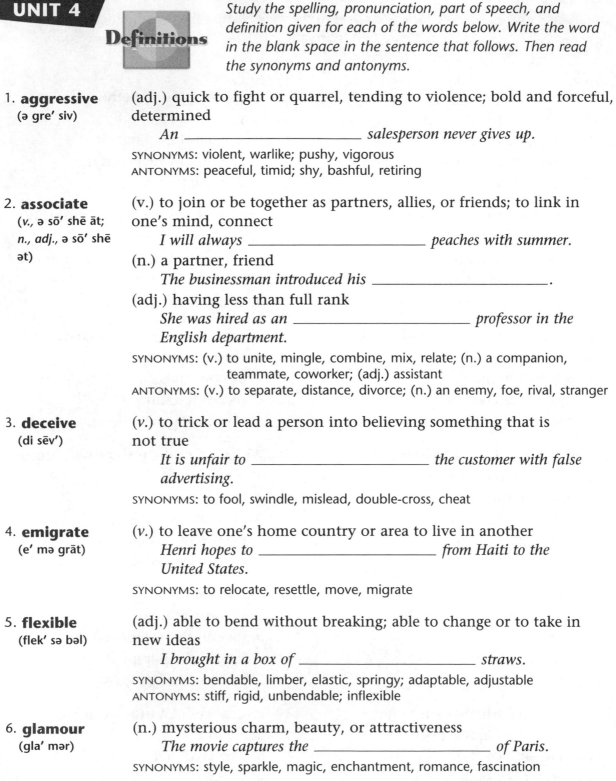

Definitions

Study the spelling, pronunciation, part of speech, and definition given for each of the words below. Write the word in the blank space in the sentence that follows. Then read the synonyms and antonyms.

1. **aggressive**
   (ə gre' siv)

   (adj.) quick to fight or quarrel, tending to violence; bold and forceful, determined
   An _____ salesperson never gives up.
   SYNONYMS: violent, warlike; pushy, vigorous
   ANTONYMS: peaceful, timid; shy, bashful, retiring

2. **associate**
   (*v.,* ə sō' shē āt; *n., adj.,* ə sō' shē ət)

   (v.) to join or be together as partners, allies, or friends; to link in one's mind, connect
   I will always _____ peaches with summer.
   (n.) a partner, friend
   The businessman introduced his _____.
   (adj.) having less than full rank
   She was hired as an _____ professor in the English department.
   SYNONYMS: (v.) to unite, mingle, combine, mix, relate; (n.) a companion, teammate, coworker; (adj.) assistant
   ANTONYMS: (v.) to separate, distance, divorce; (n.) an enemy, foe, rival, stranger

3. **deceive**
   (di sēv')

   (v.) to trick or lead a person into believing something that is not true
   It is unfair to _____ the customer with false advertising.
   SYNONYMS: to fool, swindle, mislead, double-cross, cheat

4. **emigrate**
   (e' mə grāt)

   (v.) to leave one's home country or area to live in another
   Henri hopes to _____ from Haiti to the United States.
   SYNONYMS: to relocate, resettle, move, migrate

5. **flexible**
   (flek' sə bəl)

   (adj.) able to bend without breaking; able to change or to take in new ideas
   I brought in a box of _____ straws.
   SYNONYMS: bendable, limber, elastic, springy; adaptable, adjustable
   ANTONYMS: stiff, rigid, unbendable; inflexible

6. **glamour**
   (gla' mər)

   (n.) mysterious charm, beauty, or attractiveness
   The movie captures the _____ of Paris.
   SYNONYMS: style, sparkle, magic, enchantment, romance, fascination

For vocabulary games and activities, visit **www.sadlier-oxford.com**.

The main **span** (word 12) of the Golden Gate Bridge is 4,200 feet in length. When it was completed in 1937, it was the longest suspension bridge in the world.

7. **hazy**
(hā′ zē)

(adj.) unclear, misty; not readily seen or understandable

Another hot and _____ day is forecast.

SYNONYMS: cloudy, smoggy, foggy, blurry, dim; vague
ANTONYMS: bright, clear; precise

8. **linger**
(liŋ′ gər)

(v.) to stay longer than expected, be slow in leaving; to go slowly or take one's time

We like to _____ over breakfast on Saturdays.

SYNONYMS: to delay, stall, remain, stay, lag, persist; to dawdle
ANTONYMS: to hurry, rush, charge, hasten

9. **luxurious**
(ləg zhùr′ ē əs)

(adj.) providing ease and comfort far beyond what is ordinary or necessary

They took a _____ vacation.

SYNONYMS: rich, elegant, pleasurable, lavish, extravagant, fancy
ANTONYMS: poor, plain, simple, modest

10. **mishap**
(mis′ hap)

(n.) an unfortunate but minor accident

The waiters chuckled over the _____.

SYNONYMS: a misfortune, mistake, blunder, slipup

11. **overwhelm**
(ō vər welm′)

(v.) to overcome by superior force, crush; to affect so deeply as to make helpless

Fresh troops threatened to _____ the weakened defenders.

SYNONYMS: to overpower, destroy, crush; to stun, shock, stagger, astound

12. **span**
(span)

(n.) the full reach or length, especially between two points in space or time

The _____ of most insects' lives is very brief.

(v.) to stretch or reach across

A new bridge will be built to _____ the river.

SYNONYMS: (n.) extent, distance, length, scope, period; (v.) to bridge, cross, last

Match the Meaning

For each item below, choose the word whose meaning is suggested by the clue given. Then write the word in the space provided.

1. People who are too _____ often get into quarrels or fights.
   a. flexible   b. hazy   c. luxurious   d. aggressive

2. To fool people into believing what is not true is to _____ them.
   a. overwhelm   b. deceive   c. emigrate   d. linger

3. If you join with me as a partner, you _____ with me.
   a. associate   b. deceive   c. overwhelm   d. span

4. It is not easy to see distant mountains on a(n) _____ day.
   a. aggressive   b. flexible   c. hazy   d. luxurious

5. A princess's charm and beauty might make her a symbol of _____.
   a. associate   b. mishap   c. span   d. glamour

6. To _____ from Korea to Nepal is to leave Korea to live in Nepal.
   a. associate   b. emigrate   c. linger   d. overwhelm

7. Getting a paper cut is an example of a minor _____.
   a. mishap   b. span   c. associate   d. glamour

8. A mighty army might easily _____ a weaker foe.
   a. emigrate   b. linger   c. overwhelm   d. associate

9. A(n) _____ straw makes it easy to drink from a juice box.
   a. luxurious   b. aggressive   c. flexible   d. hazy

10. A _____ hotel might provide six fluffy bath towels for each guest.
    a. aggressive   b. hazy   c. flexible   d. luxurious

11. To stay longer than expected or to leave slowly is to _____.
    a. deceive   b. linger   c. emigrate   d. span

12. A bridge that crosses the Mississippi is said to _____ that river.
    a. span   b. associate   c. linger   d. overwhelm

Synonyms

*For each item below, choose the word that is most nearly the **same** in meaning as the word or phrase in **boldface**. Then write your choice on the line provided.*

1. the **magic** of Hollywood
   a. mishap   b. span   c. glamour   d. associate   _____

2. **crush** our opponents
   a. deceive   b. emigrate   c. linger   d. overwhelm   _____

3. told us about the **slipup**
   a. glamour   b. span   c. mishap   d. associate   _____

4. **move** from Egypt to Italy
   a. overwhelm   b. linger   c. deceive   d. emigrate   _____

5. **mislead** the enemy
   a. associate   b. deceive   c. overwhelm   d. emigrate   _____

6. over the **period** of a year
   a. associate   b. mishap   c. span   d. glamour   _____

Antonyms

*For each item below, choose the word that is most nearly **opposite** in meaning to the word or phrase in **boldface**. Then write your choice on the line provided.*

1. **timid** base runners
   a. associate   b. aggressive   c. luxurious   d. hazy   _____

2. introduced her **rival**
   a. glamour   b. associate   c. span   d. mishap   _____

3. **hurry** over our good-byes
   a. span   b. emigrate   c. overwhelm   d. linger   _____

4. a **rigid** point of view
   a. flexible   b. aggressive   c. hazy   d. luxurious   _____

5. a **simple** meal with friends
   a. aggressive   b. flexible   c. luxurious   d. hazy   _____

6. a **clear** sky
   a. flexible   b. luxurious   c. aggressive   d. hazy   _____

Completing the Sentence

From the list of words on pages 30–31, choose the one that best completes each item below. Then write the word in the space provided. (You may have to change the word's ending.)

A NEW LIFE IN AMERICA

■ Poor conditions in their homeland have driven many Mexicans to _____ to the United States. Many have settled in the Southwest, but others have traveled to big cities in the Midwest and Northeast in search of work.

■ Some dishonest agents _____ travelers by taking their money in exchange for legal documents that they never provide.

■ Over the _____ of the past fifty years, more immigrants have come to the United States from Mexico than from any other country.

■ Many immigrants have only a(n) _____ notion of what life will be like in the new country they have heard so much about.

■ Mix-ups over language or local customs often lead to _____ and misunderstandings.

■ Despite facing some _____ problems, most immigrants manage to build better lives for themselves and their families.

A LEGAL BRIEF

■ It is a lawyer's duty to act in a(n) _____ fashion in order to protect the interests of his or her clients. Trial lawyers especially cannot afford to be timid or shy.

■ Most lawyers, like other professionals, have to keep _____ hours in order to serve their clients well.

■ From the newest _____ to senior partners, lawyers must research past cases to find ways to support their arguments. For this reason they often spend long hours in law libraries.

■ Media attention lends some legal cases more _____ than they really deserve. Some especially newsworthy trials are now televised from start to finish.

■ The impact of such cases may _____ in the public mind long after all the lawyers, the judge, and the jurors have left the courtroom.

■ Lawyers on television and in movies are often seen to drive _____ cars and wear expensive clothes. In fact, most real-life lawyers work long, hard hours and rarely enjoy the spotlight of celebrity.

 **Word Associations** *Circle the letter next to the word or expression that best completes the sentence or answers the question. Pay special attention to the word in* **boldface.**

1. Which is an example of a **mishap**?
   a. solving a riddle
   b. a serious car accident
   c. stepping in a puddle
   d. telling a lie

2. If a movie **overwhelms** you, you
   a. might feel like you will cry
   b. might ask for a refund
   c. might refuse to clap
   d. might get very hungry

3. If you have a **hazy** grasp of map reading, you should
   a. use a brighter lamp
   b. memorize the state capitals
   c. take the bus
   d. learn more about keys and symbols

4. You might **linger** if you are
   a. not wearing a watch
   b. late for an appointment
   c. having a great time
   d. bored to tears

5. A **luxurious** outfit might include
   a. gold jewelry
   b. rags
   c. T-shirts
   d. aluminum foil

6. Which would most people **associate**?
   a. bicycles with snowshoes
   b. winter with fireworks
   c. fishing with homework
   d. vacations with summer

7. In a place known for **glamour,** a visitor might find
   a. cows grazing in a field
   b. unpaved roads
   c. lots of factories
   d. expensive restaurants

8. **Aggressive** ballplayers would
   a. lose interest in the game
   b. play as hard as they can
   c. let their opponents win
   d. ask to sit out the game

9. You might **deceive** a puppy by
   a. pretending to throw a ball
   b. taking off its collar
   c. feeding it twice a day
   d. changing your clothes

10. A U.S. citizen might **emigrate** to
    a. the moon
    b. Florida
    c. Canada
    d. New York City

11. The "**span** of a lifetime" means
    a. from Monday to Friday
    b. from birth to death
    c. from kindergarten to college
    d. from breakfast to dinner

12. Which is the most **flexible**?
    a. a frying pan
    b. a pipe wrench
    c. an extension ladder
    d. a garden hose

For vocabulary games and activities, visit www.sadlier-oxford.com.

Selecting Word Meanings

For each of the following items, circle the choice that is most nearly the **same** in meaning as the word in **boldface.**

1. a **myth** about the beginning of Rome
   a. fact   b. legend   c. trial   d. doubt

2. a **flexible** kind of plastic
   a. rigid   b. fireproof   c. elastic   d. slippery

3. **deceived** his partner
   a. honored   b. amused   c. soothed   d. double-crossed

4. a witness to the **assault**
   a. attack   b. accident   c. joke   d. agreement

5. **overwhelm** the enemy
   a. entertain   b. crush   c. outrun   d. trick

6. **reject** the application
   a. study   b. accept   c. forget   d. decline

7. climbed the **bluff**
   a. stairs   b. tower   c. bank   d. ladder

8. a **haven** for travelers
   a. map   b. show   c. refuge   d. tour

9. **linger** near home
   a. remain   b. play   c. hide   d. dig

10. **despise** cruelty to animals
    a. admire   b. outlaw   c. detest   d. fear

11. **abandon** the house
    a. build   b. occupy   c. desert   d. watch

12. a **vivid** picture
    a. small and blurry   b. dark and gloomy   c. bright and colorful   d. famous and expensive

Spelling

*For each item below, study the **boldface** word in which there is a blank. If a letter is missing, fill in the blank to make a correctly spelled word. If the word is already spelled correctly, leave the blank empty.*

1. **em__grate** from India

2. a **min__ature** poodle

3. **stra__gle** into class

4. a sudden **mis__ap**

5. a government **do__ument**

6. a confusing **strate__gy**

7. **con__ist** of bread and water

8. a **solit__ry** ladybug

9. an **impres__ive** score

10. **span__** the stream

11. a **tempor__ry** arrangement

12. the sneaky **vi__lain**

Antonyms

*For each of the following items, circle the choice that is most nearly the **opposite** in meaning to the word in **boldface**.*

1. a **continuous** line
   a. short   b. thin   c. broken   d. thick

2. **justify** my decision to move
   a. defend   b. explain   c. question   d. regret

3. **veteran** tournament players
   a. inexperienced   b. skilled   c. popular   d. seasoned

4. **numerous** students
   a. many   b. happy   c. angry   d. few

5. a **productive** day
   a. cool   b. fruitful   c. inactive   d. memorable

6. turned out to be an **obstacle**
   a. advantage   b. enemy   c. problem   d. echo

7. **postpone** a decision
   a. delay   b. hasten   c. question   d. change

8. a **hazy** memory of the accident
   a. sad   b. dim   c. disturbing   d. clear

Vocabulary for Comprehension

*Read the following passage in which some of the words you have studied appear in **boldface**. Then answer the questions on page 39.*

The Tallest Sailor in the World

A thunderous wave crashed on Cape Cod. A loud cry split the air, and the worried villagers rushed to the beach. What they saw **overwhelmed** them. The noise had come from a **solitary** baby—a baby who was 6 feet tall! The locals put the giant baby in a cart and hauled him into town. They named him Alfred Bulltop Stormalong but called him Stormy.

Stormy grew to love the sea. He loved swimming in the deep water and riding the sea monsters. He was fearless. Once he even turned an abandoned house upside down and tried to sail away in it.

Stormy grew to be 36 feet tall, and Cape Cod became too small. **Abandoning** Cape Cod, Stormy traveled to Boston. There he joined some sailors on a huge sailing vessel. Stormy was no ordinary crewmember. He ate stew from a rowboat, and he slept wrapped in the mainsail. The sailors were in awe of him. Before long, Stormy proved his ability and usefulness to the sailors.

Stormalong's sailing skills were **impressive**, too. In one adventure, Stormy was sailing *The Courser* through the English Channel when he discovered that the waterway was only 6 inches wider than *The Courser*. Expecting a tight fit, Stormy told the crew to soap the sides of the ship. *The Courser* slipped through, but not without **mishap**. The huge ship scraped the Dover Cliffs, leaving behind a thick layer of soap. These cliffs have been pure white ever since. Folks there say that the Channel is still foamy from the soap.

Fill in the circle next to the choice that best completes the sentence or answers the question.

1. This passage is mostly about
   a the work sailors do
   b how to become a sailor
   c life in old New England
   d one unusual sailor

2. The meaning of **overwhelmed** is
   a astounded
   b exhausted
   c amused
   d useless

3. In this passage, **solitary** means
   a friendly
   b temporary
   c just one
   d tiny

4. Alfred Bulltop Stormalong spent most of his time
   a in Boston
   b near or at sea
   c far inland
   d on *The Courser*

5. Stormy was different from the other sailors because
   a he was less experienced than they were
   b he was a hated villain
   c he was sensitive and fragile
   d he was very tall

6. In this passage, the meaning of **abandoning** is
   a visiting
   b forsaking
   c occupying
   d crossing

7. **Impressive** most nearly means
   a commanding attention
   b fading away
   c plentiful
   d continuous

8. What was *The Courser*?
   a a submarine
   b a battleship
   c a sailing ship
   d a fishing boat

9. Another word for **mishap** is
   a reminder
   b scuffle
   c accident
   d spin

10. According to the passage, what made the Dover Cliffs white?
   a chalk
   b sand
   c sea foam
   d soap

 **Grammar in Context**

A **run-on sentence** is two or more sentences that run together. When you read a run-on sentence, it is hard to tell where one idea ends and a new one begins.

He ate stew from a rowboat he slept wrapped in the mainsail. ← **run-on sentence**

To fix a run-on sentence:

- Rewrite the sentence as two separate sentences.

    He ate stew from a rowboat. He slept wrapped in the mainsail.

    OR

- Rewrite the sentence as a compound sentence. Add a comma and the conjunction *and*, *but*, or *or* to join the sentences.

    He ate stew from a rowboat, <u>and</u> he slept wrapped in the mainsail.

Fix each run-on sentence. Write it as two separate sentences, or rewrite it as a compound sentence.

1. It was a hot and hazy day Stormy was ready to set sail. _____

   _____

2. Stormy knew that the seas could be treacherous he was not afraid. _____

   _____

3. The sailors pulled hard on the anchor numerous times it did not budge. _____

   _____

4. The veteran crew could keep tugging they could let Stormy try. _____

   _____

5. The sailors abandoned the smaller ship they built a bigger one. _____

   _____

6. Stormy went west his stay was temporary. _____

   _____

 **Completing the Idea**

*Complete each sentence so that it makes sense. Pay attention to the word in **boldface**.*

1. We had to **cancel** the picnic when _____.

2. I **associate** the month of June with _____.

3. At last, we ended the **dispute** by _____.

4. I can **justify** my actions by _____.

5. The directions were so **misleading** that I _____.

6. We had to **postpone** the game because _____.

7. I am **cautious** when I _____.

8. My favorite dessert **consists** of _____.

9. The cool shade is my **haven** when _____.

10. If I **straggle** at the airport, I might _____.

11. Dancers stay **flexible** so they can _____.

12. The photo was so **vivid** I could _____.

13. Because our dog can be **aggressive**, we _____.

14. When I imagine **glamour**, I picture _____.

15. I might **linger** in the hallway after school because _____.

Write Your Own
Choose a word from Units 1–4. Write a sentence using the word. Be sure the sentence is not a run-on.

_____

_____

Word Families

*The words in **boldface** in the sentences below are related to words introduced in Units 1–4. For example, the nouns* justification *and* cancellation *in item 1 are related to the verbs* justify *(Unit 2) and* cancel *(Unit 1). Based on your understanding of the unit words that follow, circle the related word in **boldface** that best completes each sentence.*

aggressive	associate	cancel	cautious	consist
convert	deceive	distribute	document	emigrate
flexible	glamour	justify	luxurious	myth
postpone	reject	straggle	strategy	treacherous

1. Blizzard conditions led to the (**justification/cancellation**) of flights throughout the upper Midwest.

2. Unicorns and dragons are classic examples of (**mythical/strategic**) animals.

3. The potato famine of the 1840s led to the (**flexibility/emigration**) of hundreds of thousands of Irish to the United States.

4. One should always use extreme (**caution/distribution**) when approaching a wild animal.

5. Our guide warned the (**associations/stragglers**) that they might get lost if they didn't keep up with the rest of the tour group.

6. The traitor Benedict Arnold is better known for his (**treachery/luxury**) than for his earlier service to the American cause.

7. A buyer of a painting by an Old Master will want to see some (**aggression/documentation**) that proves it is not a fake.

8. The melted ice cream tasted sweet but had the (**consistency/postponement**) of soup.

9. The downtown areas of some cities are coming to life once again thanks to the (**conversion/rejection**) of old factory buildings into shops and housing.

10. Some who go to Hollywood in search of fame and fortune find that life there is not so (**deceptive/glamorous**) as they have been led to believe.

Word Games

Use the clue and the given letters to complete each word. Write the missing letters of the word in the appropriate boxes. Then use the circled letters and the drawing to answer the CHALLENGE question below.

1. Not to be trusted

☐ ☐ E Ⓞ ☐ ☐ ☐ R ☐ ☐ ☐

2. Tending to use force or violence

☐ ☐ G ☐ ☐ S ☐ ☐ Ⓞ ☐

3. Constant or unbroken

☐ ☐ ☐ ☐ Ⓞ ☐ U ☐ U ☐

4. A brief tussle or fist fight

☐ C ☐ F ☐ Ⓞ ☐

5. A king or queen

☐ ☐ Ⓞ A ☐ ☐ H

6. Rich and elegant

Ⓞ ☐ X ☐ ☐ ☐ ☐ ☐ S

7. Mix or join with

☐ S ☐ ☐ ☐ Ⓞ ☐ ☐ E

Challenge:

What am I?

☐ ☐ ☐ ☐ ☐ ☐ ☐

Definitions

Study the spelling, pronunciation, part of speech, and definition given for each of the words below. Write the word in the blank space in the sentence that follows. Then read the synonyms and antonyms.

1. **blemish**
   (ble′ mish)

   (n.) a mark or stain that damages the appearance of something; a weakness or flaw

   The carpenter noticed a _____ in the finish of the cabinet.

   SYNONYMS: a scar, spot, smudge; a defect, weak spot

2. **blunt**
   (blunt)

   (adj.) having a dull point or edge, not sharp; honest but insensitive in manner

   My uncle gave me some _____ advice.

   (v.) to make less sharp

   Misuse will _____ a knife blade.

   SYNONYMS: (adj.) dull; outspoken, frank, direct
   ANTONYMS: (adj.) sharp, keen; tactful, diplomatic; (v.) to sharpen

3. **capable**
   (kā′ pə bəl)

   (adj.) able and prepared to do something; fit or skilled

   A _____ teacher should be rewarded.

   SYNONYM: qualified
   ANTONYMS: unqualified, incapable, unfit

4. **conclude**
   (kən klüd′)

   (v.) to finish; to bring something to an end; to decide after careful thought

   After electing a new secretary, the committee voted to _____ the meeting.

   SYNONYMS: to close, complete, stop; to reason, judge
   ANTONYMS: to open, begin, start, commence

5. **detect**
   (di tekt′)

   (v.) to find or discover something, notice

   A test may _____ chemicals in the water supply.

   SYNONYMS: to observe, spot
   ANTONYMS: to miss, overlook

6. **fatigue**
   (fə tēg′)

   (n.) weariness or exhaustion from work or lack of sleep

   By the end of the day I felt overcome with _____.

   (v.) to make very tired

   The riders were warned not to _____ the horses.

   SYNONYMS: (n.) tiredness, sleepiness, weakness; (v.) to tire
   ANTONYMS: (n.) liveliness, energy; (v.) to energize, perk up

A Bedouin is shown here leading camels across the desert. Bedouins are **nomads** (word 9) who speak Arabic and live in the Middle East.

7. **festive**
(fes′ tiv)

(adj.) having to do with a feast or celebration

Decorations will help lend a _____ *atmosphere.*

SYNONYMS: happy, merry, playful
ANTONYMS: sad, gloomy, somber

8. **hospitality**
(häs pə ta′ lə tē)

(n.) a friendly welcome and treatment of guests

The innkeepers were famous for their _____.

SYNONYMS: friendliness, generosity, warmth
ANTONYMS: unfriendliness, hostility

9. **nomad**
(nō′ mad)

(n.) a member of a people who move from place to place; a person who roams aimlessly

The adventurer lived the life of a _____.

SYNONYMS: a wanderer, roamer, rover

10. **persecute**
(pûr′ si kyüt)

(v.) to treat unjustly or cause to suffer

The dictator may try to _____ *the minority group.*

SYNONYMS: to torment, hurt, annoy
ANTONYMS: to reward, favor, comfort, help, protect

11. **supreme**
(sə prēm′)

(adj.) highest in power, rank, authority, quality, or degree

He acted as if giving up his seat were the _____ *sacrifice.*

SYNONYMS: first, greatest, dominant, outstanding
ANTONYMS: low, lowly, worst

12. **transport**
(*v.*, trans pôrt′;
n., trans′ pôrt)

(v.) to move or carry from one place to another

A mover was hired to _____ *the furniture.*

(n.) a vehicle used to move things from place to place; the act or process of moving something from one place to another

The ocean liner was used as troop _____ *during the war.*

SYNONYMS: (v.) to haul, cart, send, convey

Match the Meaning

For each item below, choose the word whose meaning is suggested by the clue given. Then write the word in the space provided.

1. People who never settle down in one place are called _____.
   a. blemishes   b. transports   c. hospitalities   d. nomads

2. To _____ someone is to be cruel to that person.
   a. conclude   b. persecute   c. blunt   d. detect

3. To prove your ability at something is to show yourself _____.
   a. capable   b. festive   c. supreme   d. blunt

4. A train is a good form of _____ if you want to enjoy the scenery.
   a. nomad   b. transport   c. blemish   d. fatigue

5. Weddings and birthdays are examples of _____ events.
   a. blunt   b. capable   c. festive   d. supreme

6. To notice something is to _____ it.
   a. detect   b. conclude   c. persecute   d. blunt

7. You can usually overcome _____ by getting a good night's sleep.
   a. transport   b. hospitality   c. fatigue   d. blemishes

8. The _____ Court is the highest in the land.
   a. Supreme   b. Blunt   c. Festive   d. Capable

9. It's a good idea to _____ a speech with a summary.
   a. blunt   b. conclude   c. detect   d. persecute

10. A smudge in a paint job is an example of a _____.
    a. hospitality   b. transport   c. nomad   d. blemish

11. Improper use of a knife may _____ its edge.
    a. detect   b. transport   c. blunt   d. conclude

12. Good hosts would be sure to show _____.
    a. transport   b. hospitality   c. blemish   d. fatigue

*For each item below, choose the word that is most nearly the **same** in meaning as the word or phrase in **boldface**. Then write your choice on the line provided.*

1. her **outstanding** accomplishment

   a. blunt   b. festive   c. supreme   d. capable   _____

2. tried to conceal the **flaw**

   a. blemish   b. nomad   c. fatigue   d. hospitality   _____

3. **carry** the grain to distant markets

   a. conclude   b. detect   c. blunt   d. transport   _____

4. a **skilled** performer, but not a star

   a. supreme   b. capable   c. blunt   d. festive   _____

5. followed the trail of **wanderers**

   a. transports   b. blemishes   c. nomads   d. hospitalities   _____

6. a **happy** atmosphere

   a. festive   b. capable   c. supreme   d. blunt   _____

Antonyms

*For each item below, choose the word that is most nearly **opposite** in meaning to the word or phrase in **boldface**. Then write your choice on the line provided.*

1. **overlook** the danger

   a. detect   b. conclude   c. persecute   d. transport   _____

2. spoke in a **diplomatic** manner

   a. supreme   b. festive   c. blunt   d. capable   _____

3. **begin** the homework project

   a. detect   b. persecute   c. transport   d. conclude   _____

4. **protected** the strangers

   a. blunted   b. persecuted   c. concluded   d. detected   _____

5. surprised by their **liveliness**

   a. nomad   b. blemish   c. fatigue   d. hospitality   _____

6. showed **unfriendliness** to the visitors

   a. fatigue   b. hospitality   c. transports   d. blemishes   _____

 **Completing the Sentence**

From the list of words on pages 44–45, choose the one that best completes each item below. Then write the word in the space provided. (You may have to change the word's ending.)

SPEAKING OUT AGAINST BIAS

■ The principal did not mince her words but spoke in _____ terms on the subject of prejudice to the students assembled in the school auditorium.

■ She described the ugly insult that had been written on a wall as a _____ on the school's honor.

■ She went on to warn that she would not allow a handful of students to be _____ just because they held different religious beliefs from most.

■ "Sometimes it requires a _____ effort," she said, "to overcome our prejudices and respect the diginity of others. But it is an effort that all civilized people must make."

■ She asked that everyone work together to make ours a school that is known for the _____ it shows to all.

ON THE MOVE

■ Though many Native American peoples lived in settled villages and tilled the land, many others lived the life of _____.

■ The nomadic tribes of the Great Plains marked successful buffalo hunts with _____ ceremonies of thanks.

■ In Asia the nomadic Kazakhs use camels to _____ their tents, called *yurts*, and other belongings from place to place.

■ Because they lose body water very slowly, camels are _____ of traveling for days, even in extreme heat, without drinking a drop. When they do have water to drink, they can consume as much as 25 gallons in ten minutes!

A TRAIN DERAILS

■ The safety panel looking into the train crash _____ that the most likely cause was human error.

■ It was learned that the engineer had not slept in over 36 hours and was probably suffering from extreme _____.

■ Furthermore, tests of the equipment did not _____ any signs of failure in the train's braking system.

 **Word Associations**

*Circle the letter next to the word or expression that best completes the sentence or answers the question. Pay special attention to the word in **boldface**.*

1. If you feel **fatigue**, you might
   a. take a nap
   b. run 3 miles
   c. swim 50 laps
   d. clean out the garage

2. Which *cannot* offer **hospitality**?
   a. a school
   b. a gift box
   c. a town
   d. a person

3. Someone who is **blunt** might
   a. cheer you up
   b. hurt your feelings
   c. lie to you
   d. forget your birthday

4. Which is a **festive** event?
   a. a final exam
   b. a terrible tragedy
   c. a birthday party
   d. a criminal trial

5. A **capable** student is one who
   a. travels a long way to school
   b. misses a lot of school
   c. does well in school
   d. knows everyone in school

6. Which of the following might you use to **detect** something?
   a. a pencil
   b. a magnifying glass
   c. a sandwich
   d. a pair of scissors

7. A **blemished** jewel will probably
   a. cost less than a flawless one
   b. be stolen
   c. be found in a museum
   d. cost more than a flawless one

8. A good detective might **conclude** a robbery case by
   a. turning in her badge
   b. looking for clues
   c. having donuts and coffee
   d. arresting the thief

9. Your **supreme** achievement is
   a. your greatest
   b. your worst
   c. your first
   d. your last

10. A **nomad's** home might be
    a. an apartment
    b. a castle
    c. a tent
    d. a farmhouse

11. If I were **persecuted,** I would
    a. feel happy
    b. feel hungry
    c. feel hurt
    d. feel sleepy

12. Which might **transport** an elephant?
    a. a skateboard
    b. a shopping cart
    c. a hot-air balloon
    d. a big truck

Definitions

Study the spelling, pronunciation, part of speech, and definition given for each of the words below. Write the word in the blank space in the sentence that follows. Then read the synonyms and antonyms.

1. **accomplish**
   (ə käm' plish)

   (v.) to do, make happen, succeed in, carry through
   Let's work together to _____ the task.

   SYNONYMS: to perform, fulfill, achieve, complete
   ANTONYMS: to fail, undo, fall short

2. **apparent**
   (ə par' ənt)

   (adj.) open to view; easy to understand; seeming to be true or real
   Speeding was the _____ cause of the accident.

   SYNONYMS: clear, obvious, visible; plain; likely
   ANTONYMS: hidden, concealed; difficult, uncertain

3. **capacity**
   (kə pa' sə tē)

   (n.) the amount of space that can be filled; ability or skill; office or role
   The stadium was filled to _____ for the championship game.

   SYNONYMS: volume, size, room; gift; position, job

4. **civilian**
   (sə vil' yən)

   (n.) a person not on active duty in a military, police, or firefighting force
   A team of _____ investigated the accident.
   (adj.) nonmilitary
   No _____ casualties were reported.

   SYNONYM: (n. & adj.) nonmilitary
   ANTONYM: (n. & adj.) military

5. **conceal**
   (kən sēl')

   (v.) to hide or keep secret, to place out of sight
   I tried to _____ my disappointment with a smile.

   SYNONYMS: to cover, disguise, mask, tuck away
   ANTONYMS: to uncover, open, reveal

6. **duplicate**
   (*v.,* dü' pli kāt;
   n., adj., dü' pli kət)

   (v.) to copy exactly; to produce something equal to
   A locksmith can _____ almost any key.
   (adj.) exactly like something else
   My friend and I came up with _____ plans.
   (n.) an exact copy
   He hung up a framed _____ of a famous painting in his office.

   SYNONYMS: (v.) to reproduce, clone; (adj.) identical; (n.) a reproduction, replica
   ANTONYM: (n.) an original

For vocabulary games and activities, visit **www.sadlier-oxford.com**.

It was a fad in the 1960s to test the **capacity** (word 3) of little cars by seeing how many people could fit inside them.

7. **keen**
(kēn)

(adj.) having a sharpened edge; quick and sharp in thought or in sight, hearing, or smell; eager
> *Birds of prey have _____ eyesight.*

SYNONYMS: razor-edged; acute, alert; ready
ANTONYMS: dull, blunt; lazy, unwilling

8. **provoke**
(prə vōk')

(v.) to annoy or make angry, stir up; to do something in order to get a response
> *Name-calling is bound to _____ an argument.*

SYNONYMS: to excite, enrage, madden, goad
ANTONYMS: to calm, soothe, pacify, quiet

9. **spurt**
(spûrt)

(v.) to shoot out quickly in a stream; to show a burst of energy
> *We watched the runners _____ for the finish line.*

(n.) a sudden, short stream of fluid; a quick burst of activity
> *My shirt was stained by a _____ of ketchup.*

SYNONYMS: (v.) to squirt, gush, flow; (n.) a jet, surge

10. **undoing**
(ən dü' iŋ)

(n.) a bringing to ruin or destruction; the cause of ruin; unfastening or loosening
> *Idle gossip was the cause of their _____.*

SYNONYMS: downfall, misfortune, trouble; an opening
ANTONYMS: good luck, fortune, success; fastening

11. **vast**
(vast)

(adj.) very great or very large
> *A _____ desert stretched into the distance.*

SYNONYMS: huge, enormous, spacious
ANTONYMS: tiny, small, little, narrow

12. **withdraw**
(with drô')

(v.) to pull out or remove; to move back or away, retreat
> *Is it too late to _____ from the race?*

SYNONYMS: to subtract; to leave, depart
ANTONYMS: to deposit, enter; to attack

Match the Meaning

For each item below, choose the word whose meaning is suggested by the clue given. Then write the word in the space provided.

1. Your teacher might use a copier to _____ an assignment.
   a. provoke   b. duplicate   c. accomplish   d. spurt

2. A person who is not part of the military is a(n) _____.
   a. civilian   b. capacity   c. spurt   d. undoing

3. To remove something is to _____ it.
   a. provoke   b. conceal   c. withdraw   d. duplicate

4. The number of people who can fit into a room depends upon its
   _____.
   a. capacity   b. spurts   c. duplicates   d. civilians

5. Something that seems obvious is said to be _____.
   a. keen   b. vast   c. apparent   d. civilian

6. A(n) _____ from a garden hose might get you wet.
   a. undoing   b. duplicate   c. spurt   d. capacity

7. A(n) _____ blade will cut much better than a dull one.
   a. keen   b. apparent   c. vast   d. civilian

8. If you tease someone, you might _____ that person.
   a. accomplish   b. conceal   c. provoke   d. withdraw

9. A serious mistake might lead to one's _____.
   a. capacity   b. spurt   c. civilian   d. undoing

10. To hide something is to _____ it.
    a. accomplish   b. conceal   c. provoke   d. withdraw

11. The Atlantic Ocean is a(n) _____ body of water.
    a. keen   b. duplicate   c. apparent   d. vast

12. When you reach your goal, you have _____ something.
    a. concealed   b. withdrawn   c. duplicated   d. accomplished

Synonyms

*For each item below, choose the word that is most nearly the **same** in meaning as the word or phrase in **boldface.** Then write your choice on the line provided.*

1. create an **identical** set of plans
   a. vast   b. duplicate   c. keen   d. apparent   _____

2. measured the trunk's **room**
   a. capacity   b. spurt   c. civilian   d. undoing   _____

3. **complete** the mission in two weeks
   a. provoke   b. duplicate   c. accomplish   d. withdraw   _____

4. led to the **downfall** of the dictator
   a. civilian   b. spurt   c. capacity   d. undoing   _____

5. **depart** from the battlefield
   a. withdraw   b. provoke   c. spurt   d. conceal   _____

6. water that **squirted** from the hose
   a. concealed   b. spurted   c. withdrew   d. provoked   _____

Antonyms

*For each item below, choose the word that is most nearly **opposite** in meaning to the word or phrase in **boldface.** Then write your choice on the line provided.*

1. **hidden** reasons
   a. apparent   b. keen   c. civilian   d. vast   _____

2. a **military** operation
   a. apparent   b. civilian   c. keen   d. vast   _____

3. a **small** field
   a. keen   b. duplicate   c. civilian   d. vast   _____

4. **calm** the animal
   a. provoke   b. conceal   c. duplicate   d. accomplish   _____

5. **reveal** the answers
   a. duplicate   b. provoke   c. conceal   d. withdraw   _____

6. a **dull** sense of humor
   a. vast   b. civilian   c. duplicate   d. keen   _____

Completing the Sentence

From the list of words on pages 50–51, choose the one that best completes each item below. Then write the word in the space provided. (You may have to change the word's ending.)

REVOLUTION IN AMERICA AND FRANCE

■ One of the events that led to the American Revolution was the Boston Massacre, when British soldiers fired into a crowd of _____.

■ Some historians say that the soldiers were _____ into firing by the insults and taunts of the crowd.

■ It soon became _____ to the British—even those who preferred not to see it—that the American colonies would settle for nothing less than full independence.

■ The leaders of the French Revolution were inspired by the American Revolution and hoped to _____ its success.

■ The Revolution in France led to the death of King Louis and the _____ of the old order.

A CALIFORNIA DESERT

■ With an area of 25,000 square miles, the Mojave Desert covers a(n) _____ portion of southern California. On the desert's border is Death Valley, the lowest point in North America.

■ During the daytime some animals, such as the kangaroo rat, _____ from the hot desert floor to cooler underground burrows.

■ Though the desert roadrunner is a poor flier, it can run in quick _____ to capture its prey. The roadrunner feeds on lizards, snakes, and insects.

THE SIXTEENTH PRESIDENT

■ In his _____ as commander in chief, Abraham Lincoln played an important part in choosing the generals of the Union armies.

■ One of Lincoln's choices was Ulysses S. Grant, who _____ what no other Union general before him had been able to do—force the surrender of Robert E. Lee.

■ Lincoln's aides so feared for his safety that they often went to great lengths to _____ his movements.

■ The many examples of his jokes and stories show that Lincoln possessed a(n) _____ sense of humor.

Word Associations

*Circle the letter next to the word or expression that best completes the sentence or answers the question. Pay special attention to the word in **boldface**.*

1. To **duplicate** a recipe, you might
   a. change it
   b. copy it
   c. memorize it
   d. hide it

2. When you **provoke** someone, that person is likely
   a. to thank you
   b. to forget you
   c. to be angry with you
   d. to praise you

3. Which is a **vast** distance?
   a. between Earth and Mars
   b. between your ears
   c. between footsteps
   d. between telephone poles

4. To **accomplish** something, you must
   a. think negative thoughts
   b. have lunch
   c. start at the beginning
   d. forget about it

5. You might **conceal** yourself
   a. in a chair
   b. on a busy sidewalk
   c. in a closet
   d. on top of your desk

6. Which is *not* a **civilian**?
   a. a teacher
   b. a lawyer
   c. a police officer
   d. a plumber

7. If you feel a **spurt** of energy, you
   a. might run faster
   b. might take a nap
   c. might go to the doctor
   d. might take a vitamin

8. People who have **keen** hearing
   a. can barely hear a loud siren
   b. need to have their ears examined
   c. would talk loudly
   d. can hear a pin drop

9. One of the things about you that is most **apparent** is
   a. your birthday
   b. the number of siblings you have
   c. the color of your hair
   d. whether or not you have a pet

10. You might measure the **capacity** of
    a. a bathtub
    b. a shower curtain
    c. a bar of soap
    d. a bath mat

11. Which might be a diet's **undoing**?
    a. lots of willpower
    b. lots of exercise
    c. lack of desserts
    d. lack of willpower

12. When a turtle **withdraws** its head, it
    a. wants you to pet its head
    b. pulls its head into its shell
    c. stretches its neck
    d. is ready to race

Definitions

Study the spelling, pronunciation, part of speech, and definition given for each of the words below. Write the word in the blank space in the sentence that follows. Then read the synonyms and antonyms.

1. **barrier**
   (bar′ ē ər)

   (n.) something that blocks the way; an obstacle

   Volunteers worked feverishly to build a _____ that would keep the forest fire from spreading.

   SYNONYMS: an obstruction, fence, wall, blockade, safeguard
   ANTONYMS: an opening, passage

2. **calculate**
   (kal′ kyə lāt)

   (v.) to find out by using mathematics, reckon; to find out by reasoning, estimate

   The math teacher asked us to _____ the number of hours we spend on homework each week.

   SYNONYMS: to gauge, figure, determine, judge

3. **compose**
   (kəm pōz′)

   (v.) to be or make up the parts of, form; to create or write; to calm or quiet one's mind

   Before you _____ the essay, you might write an outline.

   SYNONYMS: to produce, invent; to still, settle
   ANTONYMS: to annoy, disturb

4. **considerable**
   (kən sid′ ər ə bəl)

   (adj.) fairly large in size or extent; worthy of attention

   It will take a _____ amount of time to complete the science project.

   SYNONYMS: great, sizable, major, important
   ANTONYMS: small, slight, negligible

5. **deputy**
   (de′ pyə tē)

   (n.) one chosen to help or take the place of another or to act in that person's absence

   The sheriff's first act after winning the election was to appoint a _____.

   SYNONYMS: an assistant, aide, substitute

6. **industrious**
   (in dus′ trē əs)

   (adj.) busy, working steadily

   The crew that gathered to clean up the vacant lot were as _____ as ants.

   SYNONYMS: active, occupied, energetic, untiring
   ANTONYMS: lazy, idle, loafing, slow

For vocabulary games and activities, visit **www.sadlier-oxford.com**.

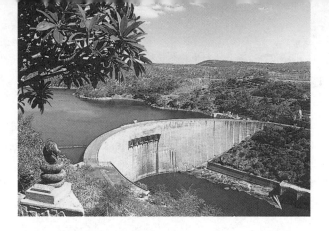

A dam is a **barrier** (word 1) constructed to control the flow of water. The dam shown here is the Kariba in the African nation of Zimbabwe.

7. **jolt**
(jōlt)

(v.) to shake up roughly; to move along in a jerky or bumpy fashion
It was fun to _____ down the dirt road in the wagon.

(n.) a sudden bump or jerk; a shock or surprise
We felt a _____ as the Ferris wheel started.

SYNONYMS: (v.) to jar, rattle, hit; (n.) a lurch, bounce

8. **loot**
(lüt)

(v.) to rob by force or violence, especially during war or time of unrest
The soldiers were warned not to _____ the villages.

(n.) valuable things that have been stolen or taken by force
Detectives found _____ from a dozen robberies.

SYNONYMS: (v.) to steal, plunder; (n.) prize, spoils

9. **rejoice**
(ri jois')

(v.) to feel joy or great delight; to make joyful
The whole town will _____ if the team wins the championship.

SYNONYMS: to celebrate, cheer
ANTONYMS: to grieve, mourn

10. **reliable**
(re lī' ə bəl)

(adj.) deserving trust, dependable
It is not easy to find a _____ babysitter.

SYNONYMS: faithful, proven, trustworthy
ANTONYMS: unreliable, questionable, fickle

11. **senseless**
(sens' ləs)

(adj.) lacking meaning, stupid or foolish; without use of the senses
The boxer was knocked _____ by the blow.

SYNONYMS: ridiculous, silly, illogical, birdbrained; unconscious
ANTONYMS: brilliant, clever, smart

12. **shrivel**
(shriv' əl)

(v.) to shrink and wrinkle, especially from heat, cold, or dryness
Exposed skin will _____ in the frosty air.

SYNONYMS: to wither, dry, contract
ANTONYMS: to expand, enlarge, swell

For each item below, choose the word whose meaning is suggested by the clue given. Then write the word in the space provided.

1. _____ people always stay busy by finding things to do.
   a. considerable   b. senseless   c. reliable   d. industrious

2. Because we forgot to water the plants, they all _____.
   a. composed   b. shriveled   c. calculated   d. rejoiced

3. When I ride my bike on an unpaved road, I feel a _____ with each bump.
   a. jolt   b. barrier   c. deputy   d. loot

4. An action without meaning may be called _____.
   a. industrious   b. considerable   c. senseless   d. reliable

5. Something that poses an obstacle is called a _____.
   a. jolt   b. deputy   c. loot   d. barrier

6. Add the cost of all the food and drinks, as well as the tax and tip, to _____ the total cost of the meal.
   a. jolt   b. calculate   c. rejoice   d. compose

7. A person chosen to act in another's absence is a _____.
   a. deputy   b. loot   c. jolt   d. barrier

8. Calm yourself and quiet your mind to _____ your thoughts.
   a. calculate   b. rejoice   c. compose   d. jolt

9. A(n) _____ number is a pretty large one.
   a. reliable   b. industrious   c. considerable   d. senseless

10. A(n) _____ car starts up every morning, even in winter.
    a. industrious   b. senseless   c. considerable   d. reliable

11. To celebrate with delight is to _____.
    a. shrivel   b. rejoice   c. calculate   d. compose

12. The robbers stashed their _____ in an old refrigerator.
    a. loot   b. barrier   c. deputy   d. jolt

Synonyms

*For each item below, choose the word that is most nearly the **same** in meaning as the word or phrase in **boldface.** Then write your choice on the line provided.*

1. knocked **unconscious** when I fell off the ladder
   a. industrious   b. senseless   c. considerable   d. reliable   _____

2. **jarred** by the rough landing
   a. jolted   b. composed   c. shriveled   d. looted   _____

3. **produce** a long poem
   a. jolt   b. calculate   c. compose   d. rejoice   _____

4. call the **assistant** for help
   a. barrier   b. loot   c. deputy   d. jolt   _____

5. **determine** the cost of painting the apartment
   a. compose   b. rejoice   c. jolt   d. calculate   _____

6. would **plunder** the house while the owners were away
   a. jolt   b. compose   c. loot   d. calculate   _____

Antonyms

*For each item below, choose the word that is most nearly **opposite** in meaning to the word or phrase in **boldface.** Then write your choice on the line provided.*

1. the **idle** carpenter
   a. considerable   b. industrious   c. reliable   d. senseless   _____

2. **swell** in the heat
   a. calculate   b. jolt   c. compose   d. shrivel   _____

3. **mourn** over the election results
   a. loot   b. calculate   c. rejoice   d. shrivel   _____

4. made a **slight** difference
   a. considerable   b. industrious   c. senseless   d. reliable   _____

5. a **questionable** source of information
   a. industrious   b. considerable   c. reliable   d. senseless   _____

6. found an **opening**
   a. deputy   b. loot   c. jolt   d. barrier   _____

Completing the Sentence

From the list of words on pages 56–57, choose the one that best completes each item below. Then write the word in the space provided. (You may have to change the word's ending.)

EARTHQUAKE!

■ The powerful earthquake that hit the San Francisco Bay area on October 17, 1989, did _____ damage to the city, though not nearly so much as was done by the terrible earthquake and fire of 1906.

■ The mighty _____, which registered 7.1 on the Richter scale, shook buildings and buckled elevated highways.

■ Safety officials quickly put up _____ to keep people away from unsafe areas.

■ Scientists _____ that the loss of life and property would have been far greater if the earthquake had hit during the day instead of early evening.

A GREAT ARTIST

■ The Dutch painter Vincent van Gogh was an ambitious and _____ artist who made hundreds of paintings and drawings during his short lifetime. He moved to southern France in 1888, and there he produced many of his masterpieces. Van Gogh died in 1890 at the age of 37.

■ Van Gogh _____ at the completion of each new painting but despaired that his work never sold.

■ As the summer heat _____ the olives on the trees near his home, van Gogh wrote sad letters to his brother Theo.

■ He _____ works of great beauty that were not appreciated until after his death. Today his paintings are in museums all over the world and are sold for millions of dollars.

SIRENS IN THE NIGHT

■ When a power blackout darkened part of the city, some criminals roamed the streets. They broke windows and _____ neighborhood stores.

■ Community leaders spoke out against this _____ violence and urged people to act responsibly during the emergency.

■ Several sheriff's _____ arrived to restore order and interview witnesses to the crime spree.

■ One witness offered information about the robberies, but the police officers paid him little mind because they knew he was not _____.

Word Associations

*Circle the letter next to the word or expression that best completes the sentence or answers the question. Pay special attention to the word in **boldface**.*

1. Which is a **barrier** to success in school?
   a. poor study habits
   b. weak stomach muscles
   c. a tall fence
   d. no brothers or sisters

2. An **industrious** person could
   a. build a hen house in ten years
   b. build a dollhouse in five years
   c. build a birdhouse in one year
   d. build a doghouse in one day

3. A **deputy** would probably carry
   a. a badge
   b. a bag lunch
   c. a wrench
   d. a banner

4. It is **senseless** to try to count
   a. to one thousand
   b. change after a purchase
   c. grains of sand at the beach
   d. people ahead of you in line

5. You might **rejoice** if you
   a. found your lost dog
   b. ruined your favorite shirt
   c. failed a spelling test
   d. saw the latest comedy film

6. Which is a **considerable** sum?
   a. 30¢
   b. $1.00
   c. $5.00
   d. $5,000.00

7. If you **compose** your autobiography, you will be
   a. driving a new car
   b. writing the story of your life
   c. interviewing strangers
   d. making up a new song

8. You might feel **jolted** by
   a. a good night's sleep
   b. a delicious lunch
   c. shocking news
   d. yesterday's paper

9. People guilty of **looting** are
   a. winning a prize
   b. breaking the law
   c. running in circles
   d. taking pictures

10. A balloon would quickly **shrivel**
    a. if air leaks from it
    b. if it floats away
    c. if it gets wet
    d. if it is tied to a string

11. A **reliable** friend is one who
    a. doesn't let you down
    b. makes fun of you
    c. is never on time
    d. always makes you laugh

12. Which might be used to **calculate**?
    a. an alarm clock
    b. paper and pencil
    c. a hammer
    d. knife and fork

Definitions

Study the spelling, pronunciation, part of speech, and definition given for each of the words below. Write the word in the blank space in the sentence that follows. Then read the synonyms and antonyms.

1. **alternate**
(*v.,* ôl' tər nāt;
n., adj., ôl' tər nət)

   (v.) to do, use, or happen in successive turns; to take turns
   We chose two students to _____ in the lead role for our class play.

   (n.) a person acting or prepared to act in place of another; a substitute
   Juries usually include two or more _____.

   (adj.) happening or appearing in turns; every other; being a choice between two or more things
   The bus driver took an _____ route.

   SYNONYMS: (v.) to rotate, change; (n.) a replacement, deputy

2. **demolish**
(di mäl' ish)

   (v.) to tear down, break to pieces
   A wrecking crew arrived to _____ the old building.

   SYNONYMS: to raze, destroy, wreck, smash, level
   ANTONYMS: to construct, build, restore, mend

3. **energetic**
(e nər je' tik)

   (adj.) active and vigorous, full of energy, forceful
   Our teacher has an _____ assistant.

   SYNONYMS: hardworking, tireless, peppy
   ANTONYMS: idle, lazy, inactive

4. **enforce**
(en fôrs')

   (v.) to force obedience to
   It is the duty of the police to protect citizens and _____ the laws.

   SYNONYM: to carry out
   ANTONYMS: to overlook, abandon, disregard

5. **feat**
(fēt)

   (n.) an act or deed that shows daring, skill, or strength
   The crowd cheered when the circus strongman performed a mighty _____.

   SYNONYMS: an achievement, exploit, effort

6. **hearty**
(härt' ē)

   (adj.) warm and friendly; healthy, lively, and strong; large and satisfying to the appetite
   We all sat down to enjoy a _____ meal.

   SYNONYMS: cheerful, friendly; fit, healthy; plentiful
   ANTONYMS: insincere, phony; sickly

Sometimes explosives are used to **demolish** (word 2) structures. Here an old hotel is brought down in Atlantic City, New Jersey.

7. **mature**
(mə tùr′)

(v.) to bring to or reach full development or growth
The puppy will _____ over the summer.
(adj.) fully grown or developed
A field of _____ oats waved in the breeze.
SYNONYMS: (v.) to grow, develop, age, ripen; (adj.) complete, ripe
ANTONYMS: (adj.) immature, inexperienced, raw, green

8. **observant**
(əb zûr′ vənt)

(adj.) watchful, quick to notice; careful and diligent
An _____ guard spotted the vandals.
SYNONYMS: aware, attentive, alert, sharp; dutiful, mindful
ANTONYMS: inattentive, careless

9. **primary**
(prī′ mer ē)

(adj.) first in importance, first in time or order; basic, fundamental
Raising money was our _____ order of business.
(n.) an early election that narrows the choice of candidates who will run in a final election
The challenger won the _____.
SYNONYMS: (adj.) highest, main, prime
ANTONYMS: (adj.) secondary, last

10. **resign**
(ri zīn′)

(v.) to give up a job, an office, or a right or claim
Richard Nixon was the first President to _____ the office.
SYNONYMS: to quit, abandon, leave, surrender

11. **strive**
(strīv)

(v.) to devote much energy or effort, try hard
You must _____ to finish your homework on time.
SYNONYMS: to attempt, struggle, labor, slave, strain

12. **verdict**
(vûr′ dikt)

(n.) the decision of a jury at the end of a trial or legal case; any decision
The jury brought in a guilty _____.
SYNONYMS: a ruling, judgment, finding

For each item below, choose the word whose meaning is suggested by the clue given. Then write the word in the space provided.

1. To make people obey laws is to _____ those laws.
   a. enforce   b. alternate   c. demolish   d. strive

2. To break something to pieces is to _____ it.
   a. alternate   b. demolish   c. resign   d. mature

3. An amazing act or deed might be called a(n) _____.
   a. feat   b. verdict   c. primary   d. alternate

4. On cold mornings, my favorite breakfast is a(n) _____ bowl of hot oatmeal with brown sugar, cinnamon, and walnuts.
   a. mature   b. observant   c. hearty   d. primary

5. The decision that a jury gives at the end of a trial is called the _____.
   a. feat   b. primary   c. alternate   d. verdict

6. If you give up a job, you _____ from it.
   a. enforce   b. resign   c. mature   d. alternate

7. Something that is first in importance, first in time order, or first in another basic way is called _____.
   a. primary   b. mature   c. alternate   d. energetic

8. In most games, players take turns or _____ moves.
   a. resign   b. demolish   c. alternate   d. enforce

9. A frisky puppy can be described as _____.
   a. observant   b. energetic   c. mature   d. primary

10. If you are very _____, you'll notice the clues.
    a. primary   b. hearty   c. mature   d. observant

11. Once fruit is fully _____, it can be harvested.
    a. energetic   b. mature   c. hearty   d. alternate

12. To try very hard is to _____.
    a. strive   b. alternate   c. demolish   d. resign

Synonyms

*For each item below, choose the word that is most nearly the **same** in meaning as the word or phrase in **boldface.** Then write your choice on the line provided.*

1. handed down the **ruling**
   a. primary   b. feat   c. alternate   d. verdict   _____

2. a **cheerful** laugh that made his shoulders jiggle
   a. alternate   b. hearty   c. mature   d. observant   _____

3. read about the daring **achievement**
   a. feat   b. verdict   c. primary   d. alternate   _____

4. packed a **replacement** camera as a backup
   a. observant   b. hearty   c. primary   d. alternate   _____

5. **abandon** the job of manager
   a. alternate   b. demolish   c. strive   d. resign   _____

6. **attempt** to learn to read Japanese
   a. demolish   b. alternate   c. strive   d. resign   _____

Antonyms

*For each item below, choose the word that is most nearly **opposite** in meaning to the word or phrase in **boldface.** Then write your choice on the line provided.*

1. **construct** a covered bridge
   a. demolish   b. strive   c. alternate   d. enforce   _____

2. **idle** workers
   a. mature   b. energetic   c. observant   d. primary   _____

3. showed an **inexperienced** outlook
   a. alternate   b. hearty   c. mature   d. primary   _____

4. an **inattentive** reader
   a. alternate   b. mature   c. observant   d. hearty   _____

5. **overlook** the "No Smoking" laws
   a. alternate   b. strive   c. resign   d. enforce   _____

6. a **secondary** cause of blindness
   a. hearty   b. observant   c. primary   d. energetic   _____

Completing the Sentence

From the list of words on pages 62–63, choose the one that best completes each item below. Write the word in the space provided. (You may have to change the word's ending.)

From the list of words on pages 62–63

RAISING A NEW HOUSE

■ The storm so badly damaged the house that it was unsafe to live in. The owner decided to _____ it and build a new one.

■ It was quite a(n) _____ to tear down the house, clear the land, and build another house in only ten weeks!

■ Two crews _____ in the building work. When one finished, the other began, so that construction went on from break of day until long after the sun went down.

■ All of the workers were encouraged to _____ as hard as they could to finish the job ahead of schedule.

■ Luckily, a(n) _____ worker spotted a mistake in the building plans before it caused a delay, and the house was finished on time. The worker was rewarded for his attention and diligence.

AN AFTER-SCHOOL JOB

■ My sister says that the responsibilities of a part-time job can help teens develop into more _____ individuals.

■ The managers at Burger Barn, where she works after school, _____ three rules: be on time, be honest, and be polite.

■ As long as she follows those rules, the managers greet her each day with a cheerful smile and a _____ handshake.

TO THE POLLS!

■ The _____ election in September decided which candidates would run for state assembly in the general election in November. In the Democratic race, two politicians challenged the two-term assemblyman for a place on the ballot.

■ All three candidates had the help of many young, _____ volunteers, who worked tirelessly to get out the vote.

■ After ballots were counted, the _____ was clear: Voters wanted the two-term assemblyman to run again.

■ However, health problems in October forced him to _____ his office and pull out of the election.

 **Word Associations** *Circle the letter next to the word or expression that best completes the sentence or answers the question. Pay special attention to the word in* **boldface.**

1. Which is a **verdict**?
   a. "Thank you!"
   b. "Good morning!"
   c. "I told you so!"
   d. "Not guilty!"

2. If you and your sister **alternate** walking the dog, then you must
   a. do twice as much walking
   b. walk the dog every other time
   c. walk the dog two times in a row
   d. walk farther than your sister

3. Which is a firefighter's **feat**?
   a. polishing the fire trucks
   b. making daring rescues
   c. wearing waterproof boots
   d. cooking firehouse stew

4. Who would **enforce** a leash law?
   a. a scientist
   b. a weather forecaster
   c. a veterinarian
   d. a dogcatcher

5. People who **strive**
   a. give up easily
   b. always succeed
   c. do their very best
   d. prefer to be outdoors

6. Which is a **mature** animal?
   a. a sleepy puppy
   b. an old turtle
   c. a frisky kitten
   d. a new chick

7. An **energetic** performer might
   a. do three shows a day
   b. nap during intermission
   c. not answer fan mail
   d. sing softly

8. Which might be **resigned**?
   a. a greeting card
   b. a doctor's prescription
   c. a homework assignment
   d. a club membership

9. A **primary** concern is one that
   a. comes last
   b. comes too late
   c. comes first
   d. comes when you least expect it

10. Which might be **hearty**?
    a. a wink
    b. a laugh
    c. a sigh
    d. a whisper

11. If you are **observant,** you are
    a. wide awake
    b. daydreaming
    c. asleep
    d. distracted

12. Which would be the hardest to **demolish**?
    a. a snow fort
    b. a house made of cards
    c. a bookcase
    d. a dollhouse

 Internet

For vocabulary games and activities,
visit **www.sadlier-oxford.com**.

Selecting Word Meanings

*For each of the following items, circle the choice that is
most nearly the **same** in meaning as the word in **boldface**.*

1. asked him to **resign**
   a. accept   b. quit   c. join   d. stay

2. discovered the pirates' **loot**
   a. bones   b. weapons   c. gifts   d. stolen goods

3. **senseless** behavior
   a. foolish   b. polite   c. noble   d. unusual

4. welcomed the **nomads**
   a. workers   b. guests   c. relatives   d. wanderers

5. an **energetic** group
   a. lazy   b. lively   c. quiet   d. friendly

6. **calculate** the distance traveled
   a. figure   b. walk   c. question   d. write down

7. a courageous **feat**
   a. failure   b. battle   c. idea   d. deed

8. the **supreme** example
   a. outstanding   b. original   c. unimportant   d. personal

9. **concealed** my fears
   a. hid   b. showed   c. emphasized   d. ignored

10. explored the **vast** continent
    a. beautiful   b. frozen   c. empty   d. huge

11. **detected** by radar
    a. hidden   b. decided   c. discovered   d. photographed

12. wore **civilian** clothes
    a. new   b. military   c. party   d. nonmilitary

Spelling

*For each item below, study the **boldface** word in which there is a blank. If a letter is missing, fill in the blank to make a correctly spelled word. If the word is already spelled correctly, leave the blank empty.*

1. a **verdi__t** of not guilty

2. **jo__lted** by the earthquake

3. an **industri__us** effort

4. the aquarium's **capa__ity**

5. ask the **depu__y** mayor

6. **he__arty** applause

7. **enfor__e** the regulations

8. keep the **d__plicate**

9. an **ap__arent** mistake

10. the **festi__e** mood

11. the family's **hos__pitality**

12. **ac__omplish** a great deal

Antonyms

*For each of the following items, circle the choice that is most nearly the **opposite** in meaning to the word in **boldface.***

1. arrived at the **barrier**
   a. passage   b. obstacle   c. river   d. corner

2. a knife's **keen** edge
   a. sharp   b. rusty   c. dull   d. broken

3. **demolished** the car
   a. built   b. destroyed   c. sold   d. washed

4. showed signs of **fatigue**
   a. surprise   b. exhaustion   c. sickness   d. energy

5. a **considerable** collection of coins
   a. small   b. huge   c. valuable   d. private

6. the **spurting** water fountain
   a. gushing   b. brand-new   c. trickling   d. old

7. the writer's **primary** meaning
   a. main   b. hidden   c. secondary   d. confusing

8. **persecuted** by their neighbors
   a. hurt   b. comforted   c. questioned   d. ignored

*Read the following passage in which some of the words you have studied appear in **boldface**. Then answer the questions on page 71.*

America's First Female Doctor

Elizabeth Blackwell (1821–1910) didn't always enjoy medicine. But once she chose to become a doctor, she let nothing stop her. In the mid-1800s, medical schools did not accept female students. People believed then that women could never become **capable** doctors. This view made Elizabeth angry. She knew that many women would feel more at ease consulting a woman rather than a man about their health. Despite public opinion, she decided to follow her dream.

Elizabeth applied to dozens of medical schools, but she was rejected by each and every one. Refusing to be discouraged, Elizabeth made **alternate** plans for her education. She read thick medical textbooks on her own. She convinced an understanding doctor to be her private tutor. She never stopped working, and she never gave up hope.

Finally, in 1847, a small college in upstate New York admitted Elizabeth Blackwell into its medical program. When she got there, she learned that her acceptance was a joke. People treated her as an outsider. Teachers and classmates teased her. Others ignored her. But Elizabeth did not let such rude behavior keep her from **accomplishing** her goal. An **industrious** student, she went to her classes and studied hard. She earned the admiration of her fellow students.

In January 1849, Elizabeth Blackwell graduated at the head of her class. She became the first woman in the United States to receive a medical degree. At her graduation, she said, "It shall be the effort of my life to shed honor on this diploma." In so doing, she broke down the **barriers** that prevented women from practicing medicine.

Fill in the circle next to the choice that best completes the sentence or answers the question.

1. This passage is best described as a(n)
   ⓐ biographical sketch
   ⓑ journal entry
   ⓒ autobiographical sketch
   ⓓ tall tale

2. Another word for **capable** is
   ⓐ able
   ⓑ caring
   ⓒ outspoken
   ⓓ eager

3. Elizabeth Blackwell was rejected by dozens of medical schools because
   ⓐ she did not have good grades
   ⓑ she did not study hard enough
   ⓒ it was too challenging for her
   ⓓ medical schools did not accept women

4. The meaning of **alternate** in this passage is
   ⓐ take turns
   ⓑ a substitute
   ⓒ other
   ⓓ enormous

5. Another word for **accomplishing** is
   ⓐ abandoning
   ⓑ avoiding
   ⓒ adjusting
   ⓓ achieving

6. **Industrious** most nearly means
   ⓐ hard working
   ⓑ idle
   ⓒ interested
   ⓓ curious

7. In this passage, the meaning of **barriers** is
   ⓐ fences
   ⓑ arguments
   ⓒ obstacles
   ⓓ vehicles

8. Elizabeth Blackwell helped other women by
   ⓐ teaching women about medicine
   ⓑ specializing in women's diseases
   ⓒ opening the door to the medical profession
   ⓓ supporting women's colleges

9. Based on this passage, Elizabeth Blackwell can best be described as
   ⓐ sensitive
   ⓑ determined
   ⓒ nervous
   ⓓ curious

10. What can be learned from Elizabeth Blackwell?
    ⓐ the need for a sense of humor
    ⓑ the importance of goals
    ⓒ the meaning of friendship
    ⓓ the value of honor

 **Grammar in Context** Sometimes the subject in a sentence is a compound subject or the predicate is a compound predicate.

A **compound subject** is two or more subjects that have the same predicate. A conjunction such as *and* joins the subjects.

> <u>Teachers</u> teased her. <u>Classmates</u> teased her.
>
> <u>Teachers and classmates</u> teased her. ⟵ **compound subject**

A **compound predicate** is two or more predicates that have the same subject. A conjunction such as *and* joins the predicates.

> She <u>went to her classes</u>. She <u>studied hard</u>.
>
> She <u>went to her classes and studied hard</u>. ⟵ **compound predicate**

*Read each pair of sentences. Combine them by joining the subjects or predicates with the word **and**. Write the new sentence on the line.*

1. Elizabeth writes letters. Elizabeth composes speeches. _____

_____

2. The students work hard. The students strive to do their best. _____

_____

3. Hospitals enforce unfair rules. Clinics enforce unfair rules. _____

_____

4. Students cheer for Elizabeth. Students rejoice for Elizabeth. _____

_____

5. Friends cannot conceal their delight. Family cannot conceal their delight. _____

_____

Fill in the circle next to the choice that best completes the sentence or answers the question.

1. This passage is best described as a(n)
   a biographical sketch
   b journal entry
   c autobiographical sketch
   d tall tale

2. Another word for **capable** is
   a able
   b caring
   c outspoken
   d eager

3. Elizabeth Blackwell was rejected by dozens of medical schools because
   a she did not have good grades
   b she did not study hard enough
   c it was too challenging for her
   d medical schools did not accept women

4. The meaning of **alternate** in this passage is
   a take turns
   b a substitute
   c other
   d enormous

5. Another word for **accomplishing** is
   a abandoning
   b avoiding
   c adjusting
   d achieving

6. **Industrious** most nearly means
   a hard working
   b idle
   c interested
   d curious

7. In this passage, the meaning of **barriers** is
   a fences
   b arguments
   c obstacles
   d vehicles

8. Elizabeth Blackwell helped other women by
   a teaching women about medicine
   b specializing in women's diseases
   c opening the door to the medical profession
   d supporting women's colleges

9. Based on this passage, Elizabeth Blackwell can best be described as
   a sensitive
   b determined
   c nervous
   d curious

10. What can be learned from Elizabeth Blackwell?
   a the need for a sense of humor
   b the importance of goals
   c the meaning of friendship
   d the value of honor

Grammar in Context Sometimes the subject in a sentence is a compound subject or the predicate is a compound predicate.

A **compound subject** is two or more subjects that have the same predicate. A conjunction such as *and* joins the subjects.

Teachers teased her. Classmates teased her.

Teachers and classmates teased her. ◄——— **compound subject**

A **compound predicate** is two or more predicates that have the same subject. A conjunction such as *and* joins the predicates.

She went to her classes. She studied hard.

She went to her classes and studied hard. ◄——— **compound predicate**

*Read each pair of sentences. Combine them by joining the subjects or predicates with the word **and**. Write the new sentence on the line.*

1. Elizabeth writes letters. Elizabeth composes speeches. _____

_____

2. The students work hard. The students strive to do their best. _____

_____

3. Hospitals enforce unfair rules. Clinics enforce unfair rules. _____

_____

4. Students cheer for Elizabeth. Students rejoice for Elizabeth. _____

_____

5. Friends cannot conceal their delight. Family cannot conceal their delight. _____

_____

Completing the Idea

*Complete each sentence so that it makes sense. Pay attention to the word in **boldface**.*

1. Dad had such a **hearty** appetite that he _____.

2. The city had to **demolish** the old house because _____.

3. I am **reliable** because I always _____.

4. Among the **loot**, the police found _____.

5. It's smart to have a **duplicate** key in case you _____.

6. It **provokes** me when you say that I _____.

7. To **transport** those heavy boxes, we can _____.

8. My favorite way to **conclude** a meal is to _____.

9. If I were a **nomad**, I'd probably _____.

10. To find the **capacity** of a fish tank, you can _____.

11. If I had a **considerable** amount of time, I would _____.

12. The most amazing **feat** I ever saw was _____.

13. I will **resign** from the team if the coach _____.

14. I feel **fatigue** when I _____.

15. To show our **hospitality**, we should _____.

Write Your Own

Choose a word from Units 5–8. Write a sentence using the word. Be sure each sentence has a subject and a predicate. If you wrote a compound subject or a compound predicate, underline it.

_____

_____

Word Families

*The words in **boldface** in the sentences below are related to words introduced in Units 5–8. For example, the nouns festivity and energy in item 1 are related to the adjectives festive (Unit 5) and energetic (Unit 8). Based on your understanding of the unit words that follow, circle the related word in **boldface** that best completes each sentence.*

accomplish	alternate	blunt	calculate	capable
compose	detect	duplicate	energetic	enforce
festive	hospitality	industrious	mature	observant
provoke	reliable	supreme	transport	undoing

1. If you are going on a long hike over steep hills on a hot summer day, you will need a lot of (**festivity/energy**).

2. The Environmental Protection Agency is responsible for the (**enforcement/ duplication**) of laws passed to ensure clean air and water for all Americans.

3. For English class I wrote a (**calculation/composition**) about my family's trip to the Grand Canyon.

4. Passengers on whale-watching cruises can (**observe/undo**) whales and sometimes dolphins swimming in the open ocean.

5. The guests at a party may talk about how (**provocative/hospitable**) their hosts are to everyone.

6. Today people can choose from many different kinds of (**transportation/ detection**) to travel across the United States and around the world.

7. A computer has the (**capability/maturity**) to solve complicated mathematical problems very quickly.

8. Most bosses agree that (**bluntness/industry**) is a valuable quality in an employee.

9. My parents chose our new family car for its (**supremacy/reliability**) in all kinds of weather conditions.

10. All over the world people gather in front of television sets to watch the amazing (**accomplishments/alternatives**) of athletes at the Olympic Games.

Word Games

Go for the Gold! Find and ring the ten words from Units 5–8 that are hidden in the grid below. Then choose from these words the ones that best complete the sentences that follow. Write the words in the blanks.

S	R	E	L	I	A	B	L	E	N
T	O	P	O	S	B	L	E	M	O
R	C	C	O	N	C	E	A	L	M
I	K	O	T	K	I	M	S	T	A
V	E	N	V	L	U	I	E	A	D
E	T	C	R	O	V	S	B	W	E
A	L	L	W	N	Y	H	E	R	O
S	P	U	R	T	V	O	T	E	R
Z	O	D	U	O	F	F	E	A	T
K	E	E	N	N	D	G	Q	T	O

Countries from every continent send their finest and most _____ athletes to compete in the Olympic Games.

All the athletes who take part in the games _____ to do their very best for their countries, their teams, and themselves.

People all over the world watch the games with _____ interest.

Some athletes achieve the remarkable _____ of setting new world records.

Many athletes, such as speed skaters and marathon runners, may rely on an extra _____ of energy at the finish of their races.

By tradition, the marathon is run on the day that the Games _____.

Definitions

Choose the word from the box that matches each definition. Write the word on the line provided. The first one has been done for you.

alternate	apparent	barrier	blemish	blunder
capable	considerable	duplicate	feat	glamour
impressive	luxurious	miniature	persecute	solitary
scuffle	straggle	~~transport~~	undoing	verdict

1. to move or carry from one place to another   _____transport_____

2. a mark or stain that damages the appearance   _____

3. fairly large in size or extent   _____

4. to stray off or trail behind   _____

5. living or being alone; being the only one   _____

6. mysterious charm, beauty, or attractiveness   _____

7. having a strong effect, commanding attention   _____

8. a bringing to ruin; the cause of ruin   _____

9. to copy exactly; to produce something equal to   _____

10. to make a foolish or careless mistake   _____

11. the decision of a jury at the end of a trial   _____

12. to take turns   _____

13. able and prepared to do something; fit or skilled   _____

14. open to view; seeming to be true or real   _____

15. a very small copy, model, or painting   _____

Antonyms

*Choose the word from the box that is most nearly **opposite** in meaning to each group of words. Write the word on the line provided. The first one has been done for you.*

1. a rival, foe, enemy — associate

2. sad, gloomy, somber — _____

3. to accept, receive, take — _____

4. inexperienced, raw, green — _____

5. to reveal, uncover — _____

6. to grieve, mourn — _____

7. daring, reckless, wild — _____

8. lasting, long-lived, permanent — _____

9. shy, bashful, retiring — _____

10. to begin, start, open — _____

11. a hero, heroine, champion — _____

12. idle, lazy, inactive — _____

13. to defend, protect, resist — _____

14. to hurry, rush, hasten — _____

15. tiny, small, little — _____

16. sturdy, hardy, strong — _____

17. to admire, esteem, adore — _____

18. to expand, enlarge, swell — _____

19. faithful, trustworthy; safe — _____

20. to agree; an agreement — _____

accomplish
aggressive
assault
~~associate~~
cautious
conceal
conclude
despise
dispute
energetic
festive
fragile
haven
justify
linger
mature
reject
rejoice
senseless
shrivel
temporary
treacherous
vast
veteran
villain

Completing the Sentence

Choose the word from the box that best completes each sentence below. Write the word in the space provided. The first one has been done for you.

Group A

blunt	civilian	emigrate	hearty
hospitality	industrious	~~myth~~	resign

1. I enjoyed reading the story of Demeter and Persephone, a Greek _____myth_____ that explains summer and winter.

2. Are you familiar with Aesop's fable about the lazy grasshopper and the _____ ant?

3. My cousins in Eastern Europe hope to _____ to the United States and join the rest of the family here.

4. I wrote a note to thank you for your gracious _____ last weekend.

5. Let's give a(n) _____ welcome to our guests who have traveled so far to be with us!

Group B

cancel	compose	hazy	obstacle
reliable	strategy	vivid	withdraw

1. Before asking Mom to increase our allowance, we'll plan a(n) _____ that is sure to succeed.

2. After Dad painted the car a(n) _____ shade of green, it was easy to spot in a crowded parking lot.

3. I plan to pay you as soon as I _____ the money from the bank.

4. I have only a(n) _____ idea of what I will do during summer vacation.

5. Let's work together to _____ lyrics for a new school song.

Classifying

Choose the word from the box that goes best with each group of words. Write the word in the space provided. Then explain what the words have in common. The first one has been done for you.

capacity	~~continuous~~	convert	detect	flexible
loot	monarch	nomad	numerous	primary

1. ongoing, endless, ____continuous____

   The words are synonyms.

2. _____, conversion, convertible

   _____

3. some, a few, many, _____

   _____

4. president, dictator, _____

   _____

5. bendable, adjustable, _____

   _____

6. _____, detective, detector

   _____

7. tribe, camel, tent, _____

   _____

8. length, weight, _____

   _____

9. boot, root, hoot, _____

   _____

10. _____, middle, secondary

   _____

Analogies

In each of the following, circle the letter for the item that best completes the comparison. Then explain the relationship on the lines provided. The first one has been done for you.

1. **cautious** is to **careful** as
   a. numerous is to simple
   b. continuous is to ugly
   c. aggressive is to forceful
   d. misleading is to true

   Relationship: *"Cautious" and "careful" are synonyms; "aggressive" and "forceful" are synonyms.*

4. **mistake** is to **blunder** as
   a. obstacle is to opening
   b. glamour is to wealth
   c. myth is to history
   d. outlaw is to villain

   Relationship: _____

   _____

   _____

2. **shrewd** is to **foolish** as
   a. high is to towering
   b. happy is to sad
   c. spotless is to neat
   d. famous is to rich

   Relationship: _____

   _____

   _____

5. **monarch** is to **kingdom** as
   a. veteran is to war
   b. villain is to hero
   c. mayor is to city
   d. senator is to election

   Relationship: _____

   _____

   _____

3. **passport** is to **document** as
   a. step is to scuffle
   b. punch is to assault
   c. map is to strategy
   d. discussion is to dispute

   Relationship: _____

   _____

   _____

6. **flexible** is to **bend** as
   a. productive is to hinder
   b. hazy is to burn
   c. fragile is to break
   d. temporary is to dissolve

   Relationship: _____

   _____

   _____

7. **dependable** is to **reliable** as
   a. hearty is to sickly
   b. dry is to moist
   c. round is to circular
   d. logical is to senseless

Relationship: _____

_____

_____

_____

9. **apparent** is to **obvious** as
   a. first is to primary
   b. dull is to keen
   c. early is to late
   d. mature is to immature

Relationship: _____

_____

_____

_____

8. **begin** is to **conclude** as
   a. search is to look
   b. help is to aid
   c. remain is to stay
   d. give up is to strive

Relationship: _____

_____

_____

_____

10. **celebration** is to **rejoice** as
   a. library is to shout
   b. contest is to compete
   c. feast is to starve
   d. building is to demolish

Relationship: _____

_____

_____

_____

Challenge: Make up your own

Write a comparison using the words in the box below. (Hint: There are three possible analogies.) Then explain the relationship on the lines provided.

barracks	barrier	blemish	blunt
civilian	club	flaw	home
keen	obstacle	soldier	sword

Analogy: _____ is to _____ as _____ is to _____.

Relationship: _____

_____

_____

Building with Latin and Greek Roots

A **root** is the basic part of a word. Knowing the meanings of common word roots can often help you figure out the meanings of words with those roots.

> **port**—carry
>
> The root **port** appears in **transport**. When you **transport** something, you move or carry it from one place to another.

The words below contain the root **port**. *Study the definition of each word. Then write the word on the line in the sample sentence.*

1. **import**   to bring goods or materials into one country from another

   Many countries _____ bananas from Costa Rica.

2. **portage**   the carrying of boats or goods over land from one body of water to another

   _____ of the supplies around the lake took over a day.

3. **porter**   someone whose job it is to carry bags or other loads, as at a railroad station or in a hotel

   The _____ loaded my heavy suitcase onto the train.

4. **portfolio**   a carrying case for loose papers or drawings; briefcase

   The student brings his artwork to class in a waterproof _____.

5. **support**   to hold up; to keep from falling; to provide for; to back or uphold

   We donate money to _____ the Wildlife Center.

7. **dependable** is to **reliable** as
   a. hearty is to sickly
   b. dry is to moist
   c. round is to circular
   d. logical is to senseless

Relationship: _____

_____

_____

_____

9. **apparent** is to **obvious** as
   a. first is to primary
   b. dull is to keen
   c. early is to late
   d. mature is to immature

Relationship: _____

_____

_____

_____

8. **begin** is to **conclude** as
   a. search is to look
   b. help is to aid
   c. remain is to stay
   d. give up is to strive

Relationship: _____

_____

_____

_____

10. **celebration** is to **rejoice** as
   a. library is to shout
   b. contest is to compete
   c. feast is to starve
   d. building is to demolish

Relationship: _____

_____

_____

_____

Challenge: Make up your own

Write a comparison using the words in the box below. (Hint: There are three possible analogies.) Then explain the relationship on the lines provided.

barracks	barrier	blemish	blunt
civilian	club	flaw	home
keen	obstacle	soldier	sword

Analogy: _____ is to _____ as _____ is to _____ .

Relationship: _____

_____

_____

Building with Latin and Greek Roots

A **root** is the basic part of a word. Knowing the meanings of common word roots can often help you figure out the meanings of words with those roots.

> **port**—carry
>
> The root **port** appears in **transport**. When you **transport** something, you move or carry it from one place to another.

*The words below contain the root **port**. Study the definition of each word. Then write the word on the line in the sample sentence.*

1. **import**   to bring goods or materials into one country from another

   Many countries _____ bananas from Costa Rica.

2. **portage**   the carrying of boats or goods over land from one body of water to another

   _____ of the supplies around the lake took over a day.

3. **porter**   someone whose job it is to carry bags or other loads, as at a railroad station or in a hotel

   The _____ loaded my heavy suitcase onto the train.

4. **portfolio**   a carrying case for loose papers or drawings; briefcase

   The student brings his artwork to class in a waterproof _____.

5. **support**   to hold up; to keep from falling; to provide for; to back or **uphold**

   We donate money to _____ the Wildlife Center.

*Circle the word in **boldface** that best completes each sentence.*

1. This beautifully written essay ought to be put in your writing (**portage, portfolio**).

2. Wooden posts (**import, support**) the deck in our yard.

3. From which country do we (**import, support**) the most electronic games?

4. My grandfather worked as a (**porter, portfolio**) on the Union Pacific Railway.

5. The 10-mile (**portage, porter**) between rivers took longer than expected.

From the list of words on page 82, choose the one that best completes each sentence below. Write the word on the line provided.

1. My mother works two jobs to

_____ our family.

2. She brought along a _____ with samples of her poetry.

3. It is customary to tip the

_____ who helps you with your suitcases.

4. The gift shops _____ unique handmade pottery from Mexico.

5. For the first _____, the canoe was hauled along a 1-mile path.

Definitions

Study the spelling, pronunciation, part of speech, and definition given for each of the words below. Write the word in the blank space in the sentence that follows. Then read the synonyms and antonyms.

1. **brisk**
   (brisk)

   (adj.) energetic, lively, fast; cool and fresh
   The flag snapped and fluttered in the _____ wind.

   SYNONYMS: quick, active, peppy; refreshing, nippy
   ANTONYMS: slow, dull, sluggish

2. **cherish**
   (cher' ish)

   (v.) to feel or show great love for; to value highly; to take special care of
   Our freedom is something we should always safeguard and _____.

   SYNONYMS: to treasure, hold dear, honor; to prize, preserve
   ANTONYMS: to hate, despise, dishonor; to neglect

3. **considerate**
   (kən si' də rət)

   (adj.) showing concern for the needs or feelings of others
   If you are a _____ guest, you might be invited back.

   SYNONYMS: thoughtful, kind, giving, gracious
   ANTONYMS: thoughtless, self-centered, selfish

4. **displace**
   (dis plās')

   (v.) to force to move or flee; to move out of position
   Officials feared that the flood would _____ the villagers from their homes.

   SYNONYMS: to uproot, expel, evict, dislodge
   ANTONYMS: to settle, plant, install

5. **downfall**
   (daùn' fôl)

   (n.) a sudden fall from power or position; a sudden and heavy snow or rain
   To this day, historians argue over what caused the Roman empire's _____.

   SYNONYMS: collapse, ruin
   ANTONYMS: triumph, success

6. **estimate**
   (v., es' tə māt;
   n., es' tə mət)

   (v.) to form a rough judgment about the size, quantity, or value of something
   I would _____ the number of people at the concert at about 15,000.

   (n.) a rough calculation; a careful guess
   The mechanic gave us an _____ for the cost of the repairs.

   SYNONYMS: (v.) to figure, judge; (n.) a calculation, opinion

Internet

For vocabulary games and activities,
visit **www.sadlier-oxford.com**.

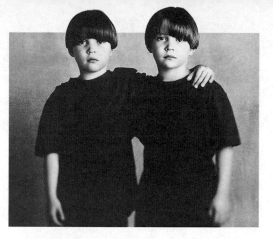

Fraternal twins may not look very much alike. But
twins who are **identical** (word 8), like those
pictured here, are usually very hard to tell apart.

7. **humiliate**
(hyü mi′ lē āt)

(v.) to hurt someone's self-respect or pride
*Our opponents accused us of trying to _____ them
by running up the score.*

SYNONYMS: to shame, disgrace, dishonor, embarrass
ANTONYMS: to honor, applaud, praise

8. **identical**
(ī den′ ti kəl)

(adj.) exactly the same, alike in every way
The twins liked to wear _____ outfits.

SYNONYM: matching
ANTONYMS: unlike, different, opposite

9. **improper**
(im prä′ pər)

(adj.) not correct; showing bad manners or taste
*The principal reminded us that _____ behavior is
not acceptable.*

SYNONYMS: incorrect, wrong; impolite, unsuitable, rude
ANTONYMS: proper, right; appropriate, polite

10. **poll**
(pōl)

(n.) a collecting of votes; (*usually plural*) a place where voting takes
place; a collecting of opinions
Where did you see the results of the _____?

(v.) to receive votes; to vote; to question people to collect opinions
*We are going to _____ our classmates about their
favorite movies.*

SYNONYMS: (n.) an election; a survey, tally; (v.) to interview, tally up

11. **soothe**
(süth)

(v.) to make calm; to ease pain or sorrow
A nurse tried to _____ the fussy child.

SYNONYMS: to quiet, pacify; to comfort, relieve
ANTONYMS: to excite, upset; to hurt, worsen

12. **vicinity**
(və si′ nə tē)

(n.) the area near a place, the surrounding region
There is a park in the _____ of our school.

SYNONYMS: neighborhood, area, surroundings

85

Match the Meaning

For each item below, choose the word whose meaning is suggested by the clue given. Then write the word in the space provided.

1. Things that look exactly alike are said to be _____.
   a. brisk   b. improper   c. identical   d. considerate

2. A heavy snowstorm would produce a(n) _____.
   a. estimate   b. poll   c. vicinity   d. downfall

3. To make an injury less painful is to _____ it.
   a. soothe   b. humiliate   c. displace   d. cherish

4. A grocery store in your neighborhood is in the _____ of your home.
   a. poll   b. vicinity   c. downfall   d. estimate

5. A cool, breezy morning might be described as _____.
   a. considerate   b. identical   c. improper   d. brisk

6. A person who is thoughtful of the feelings of others is said to be _____.
   a. considerate   b. improper   c. identical   d. brisk

7. To learn the opinions of consumers, you might _____ them.
   a. cherish   b. poll   c. displace   d. estimate

8. To take special care of something is to _____ it.
   a. poll   b. estimate   c. displace   d. cherish

9. A rough calculation is also called a(n) _____.
   a. vicinity   b. downfall   c. estimate   d. poll

10. To move something aside is to _____ it.
    a. estimate   b. displace   c. soothe   d. humiliate

11. Rude behavior might be criticized as _____.
    a. brisk   b. improper   c. considerate   d. identical

12. To embarrass or disgrace someone is to _____ that person.
    a. poll   b. soothe   c. cherish   d. humiliate

Synonyms

*For each item below, choose the word that is most nearly the **same** in meaning as the word or phrase in **boldface**. Then write your choice on the line provided.*

1. **dislodged** by the earthquake
   a. cherished   b. displaced   c. polled   d. soothed   _____

2. **embarrassed** by a failing grade
   a. cherished   b. soothed   c. humiliated   d. displaced   _____

3. **treasure** the memory of my first home run
   a. estimate   b. poll   c. cherish   d. humiliate   _____

4. **survey** voters on their choice for senator
   a. soothe   b. estimate   c. poll   d. humiliate   _____

5. recommended a restaurant in the **area**
   a. downfall   b. vicinity   c. poll   d. estimate   _____

6. **judged** the distance to be thirty feet
   a. polled   b. estimated   c. cherished   d. humiliated   _____

Antonyms

*For each item below, choose the word that is most nearly **opposite** in meaning to the word or phrase in **boldface**. Then write your choice on the line provided.*

1. the general's **triumph**
   a. downfall   b. estimate   c. poll   d. vicinity   _____

2. set a **slow** pace
   a. identical   b. brisk   c. improper   d. considerate   _____

3. held **different** views
   a. improper   b. brisk   c. identical   d. considerate   _____

4. truly **thoughtless** behavior
   a. considerate   b. brisk   c. identical   d. improper   _____

5. **worsened** the pain
   a. humiliated   b. estimated   c. polled   d. soothed   _____

6. **correct** use of the word
   a. brisk   b. considerate   c. improper   d. identical   _____

Completing the Sentence

From the list of words on pages 84–85, choose the one that best completes each item below. Then write the word in the blank space provided. (You may have to change the word's ending.)

A POLITICAL CHARGE BACKFIRES

■ In a heated speech late in the campaign, the mayor's opponent accused her of the _____ use of public funds. The mayor immediately denied the charge, declaring that she had never personally profited from her office.

■ A local newspaper conducted a _____ of likely voters. The results showed that more than 75% of those surveyed did not believe the charge leveled against the mayor.

■ Rather than be _____ by what would almost certainly be a lopsided defeat, her opponent pulled out of the race. The mayor went on to win the election by a landslide.

THE BUFFALO TRAIL

■ Before they were forcibly _____ by federal troops and European settlers, hundreds of thousands of Native Americans dwelled on the Great Plains. Among these tribes were the Blackfeet, Crow, and Sioux.

■ _____ autumn winds and deep winter snows made warm clothing and shelter essential to survival on the Great Plains. Some of these robes and the tents were made from buffalo hides.

■ Because they were so dependent upon the buffalo for food as well, many tribes never strayed very far from the _____ of the huge herds that grazed the prairie.

■ Experts _____ that as many as 30 million buffalo once roamed the vast open stretches of the northern Plains.

■ The Great Plains tribes _____ their traditions and way of life. To dishonor these customs was a serious offense.

■ The destruction of the buffalo herds in the late 1800s was one of the factors that led to the _____ of these tribes.

A FRIEND'S GOOD TURN

■ I was very upset to learn that a friend planned to come to the party in a costume _____ to mine.

■ To _____ my hurt feelings, she offered to wear a different costume instead.

■ It was very _____ of her to do that for me, don't you think?

*Circle the letter next to the word or expression that best completes the sentence or answers the question. Pay special attention to the word in **boldface**.*

1. Which of the following would you use after a **downfall**?
   a. a watering can
   b. a rake
   c. a snow shovel
   d. a hoe

2. To be **humiliated** would make you
   a. feel happy
   b. feel intelligent
   c. feel confident
   d. feel ashamed

3. If you **cherish** your pets, you
   a. will take good care of them
   b. will forget them
   c. will mistreat them
   d. will sell them

4. Which could you easily **estimate**?
   a. the height of your desk
   b. the number of seconds in a day
   c. the distance to Pluto
   d. the cost of a jumbo jet

5. Which can be **identical**?
   a. snowflakes
   b. twins
   c. fingerprints
   d. planets

6. What does one do at the **polls**?
   a. sleep
   b. learn
   c. eat
   d. vote

7. If water is **displaced**,
   a. it might freeze
   b. it might boil
   c. it might evaporate
   d. it might spill

8. For **improper** conduct, I would be
   a. scolded
   b. rewarded
   c. praised
   d. ignored

9. Which would you wear when the weather is **brisk**?
   a. a bathing suit
   b. sandals
   c. a sweater
   d. a watch

10. A **considerate** person
    a. is usually late
    b. is a poor loser
    c. is rich and famous
    d. is thoughtful of others

11. Which might be used to **soothe**?
    a. sandpaper
    b. lotion
    c. dynamite
    d. gasoline

12. In the **vicinity** of your face is
    a. your nose
    b. your toe
    c. your knee
    d. your elbow

Definitions

Study the spelling, pronunciation, part of speech, and definition given for each of the words below. Write the word in the blank space in the sentence that follows. Then read the synonyms and antonyms.

1. **abolish**
   (ə bä′ lish)

   (v.) to do away completely with something; put an end to
   Will human beings ever be able to _____ war?

   SYNONYMS: to outlaw, ban, repeal, stamp out
   ANTONYMS: to establish, restore

2. **appeal**
   (ə pēl′)

   (n.) a sincere or strong request for something that is needed; a quality or ability that attracts or interests people; a request to a higher court for review of a legal decision
   Some people don't understand the _____ of video games.

   (v.) to ask strongly for help, understanding, or something else needed; to be attractive or interesting; to request review of a legal decision
   Our class will _____ for aid for the homeless.

   SYNONYMS: (n.) a plea, petition; charm, attraction; (v.) to plead, implore, beg
   ANTONYMS: (v.) to repel, disgust, repulse

3. **brittle**
   (bri′ təl)

   (adj.) easily broken, snapped, or cracked; not flexible
   The pages of the old book had turned _____.

   SYNONYMS: breakable, stiff, unbending, fragile
   ANTONYMS: bendable, flexible, elastic, rugged

4. **condemn**
   (kən dem′)

   (v.) to criticize a person or action as wrong, guilty, or evil; to judge as guilty and to punish
   The judge is expected to _____ the defendant to life imprisonment.

   SYNONYMS: to disapprove, denounce, blame
   ANTONYMS: to praise, admire, honor, applaud, approve

5. **descend**
   (di send′)

   (v.) to move to a lower place from a higher one; to come or be handed down from the past
   We watched the climber _____ the cliff.

   SYNONYMS: to drop, fall, plunge, climb down; to stem, derive
   ANTONYMS: to rise, climb, scale, ascend

6. **dictator**
   (dik′ tā tər)

   (n.) a ruler or leader who has total power
   Sometimes my older brother acts like a _____.

   SYNONYMS: tyrant, master, despot, oppressor

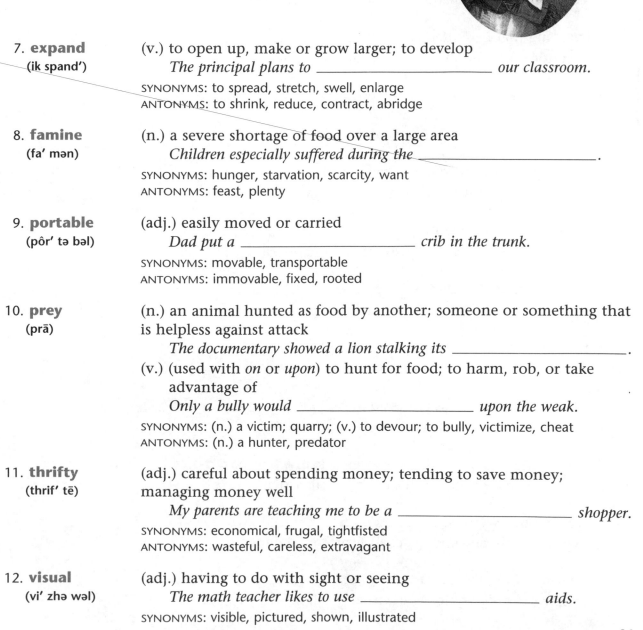

For vocabulary games and activities, visit **www.sadlier-oxford.com**.

Frederick Douglass was an escaped slave who became a leader in the movement to **abolish** (word 1) slavery. His autobiography has become a classic of American literature.

7. **expand**
(ik spand')

(v.) to open up, make or grow larger; to develop
The principal plans to _____ our classroom.

SYNONYMS: to spread, stretch, swell, enlarge
ANTONYMS: to shrink, reduce, contract, abridge

8. **famine**
(fa' mən)

(n.) a severe shortage of food over a large area
Children especially suffered during the _____.

SYNONYMS: hunger, starvation, scarcity, want
ANTONYMS: feast, plenty

9. **portable**
(pôr' tə bəl)

(adj.) easily moved or carried
Dad put a _____ crib in the trunk.

SYNONYMS: movable, transportable
ANTONYMS: immovable, fixed, rooted

10. **prey**
(prā)

(n.) an animal hunted as food by another; someone or something that is helpless against attack
The documentary showed a lion stalking its _____.

(v.) (used with *on* or *upon*) to hunt for food; to harm, rob, or take advantage of
Only a bully would _____ upon the weak.

SYNONYMS: (n.) a victim; quarry; (v.) to devour; to bully, victimize, cheat
ANTONYMS: (n.) a hunter, predator

11. **thrifty**
(thrif' tē)

(adj.) careful about spending money; tending to save money; managing money well
My parents are teaching me to be a _____ shopper.

SYNONYMS: economical, frugal, tightfisted
ANTONYMS: wasteful, careless, extravagant

12. **visual**
(vi' zhə wəl)

(adj.) having to do with sight or seeing
The math teacher likes to use _____ aids.

SYNONYMS: visible, pictured, shown, illustrated

Match the Meaning

For each item below, choose the word whose meaning is suggested by the clue given. Then write the word in the space provided.

1. To judge an action as wrong is to _____ it.
   a. condemn   b. descend   c. expand   d. abolish

2. New rooms will _____ the museum's exhibit space.
   a. condemn   b. expand   c. abolish   d. descend

3. Something that is hunted is called _____.
   a. dictator   b. famine   c. appeal   d. prey

4. An object that you can pick up and carry with you could be described as
   _____.
   a. brittle   b. visual   c. portable   d. thrifty

5. A serious food shortage might cause a(n) _____.
   a. prey   b. appeal   c. dictator   d. famine

6. To put an end to something is to _____ it.
   a. appeal   b. abolish   c. descend   d. expand

7. Something that attracts is said to have _____.
   a. appeal   b. famine   c. dictator   d. prey

8. A ruler who does not share power is a(n) _____.
   a. appeal   b. prey   c. dictator   d. famine

9. An object that snaps easily is said to be _____.
   a. visual   b. brittle   c. portable   d. thrifty

10. A _____ experience is one that has to do with sight or seeing.
   a. brittle   b. portable   c. thrifty   d. visual

11. To move downward is to _____.
   a. expand   b. descend   c. abolish   d. condemn

12. A person who looks for bargains is _____.
   a. thrifty   b. portable   c. visual   d. brittle

Synonyms

For each item below, choose the word that is most nearly the **same** in meaning as the word or phrase in **boldface.** Then write your choice on the line provided.

1. a **movable** television
   a. brittle   b. portable   c. thrifty   d. visual   _____

2. reported on the terrible **scarcity**
   a. appeal   b. prey   c. dictator   d. famine   _____

3. a powerful and selfish **tyrant**
   a. prey   b. famine   c. appeal   d. dictator   _____

4. **plead** for help
   a. abolish   b. descend   c. appeal   d. prey   _____

5. **visible** proof of the break-in
   a. visual   b. brittle   c. thrifty   d. portable   _____

6. turned **stiff** by the cold
   a. brittle   b. visual   c. portable   d. thrifty   _____

Antonyms

For each item below, choose the word that is most nearly **opposite** in meaning to the word or phrase in **boldface.** Then write your choice on the line provided.

1. **shrink** the size of the project
   a. expand   b. descend   c. appeal   d. condemn   _____

2. tracked the **predator**
   a. dictator   b. prey   c. appeal   d. famine   _____

3. **restore** the tax on medicine
   a. condemn   b. descend   c. abolish   d. expand   _____

4. **praised** the decision
   a. appealed   b. descended   c. abolished   d. condemned   _____

5. a **wasteful** consumer
   a. portable   b. visual   c. thrifty   d. brittle   _____

6. **ascend** the mountain
   a. prey upon   b. descend   c. abolish   d. expand   _____

Completing the Sentence

From the list of words on pages 90–91, choose the one that best completes each item below. Write the word in the space provided. (You may have to change the word's ending.)

AN END TO SLAVERY

■ Before the Civil War, many northerners _____ slavery as a terrible evil, but few wanted to go to war because of it. Abraham Lincoln, too, personally hated slavery but was prepared to accept it if by doing so the Union could be preserved.

■ Once the war began, however, many in the north argued that the time had come to _____ slavery once and for all. In 1863 Lincoln issued the Emancipation Proclamation, freeing slaves in the states of the Confederacy.

■ Abraham Lincoln's enemies called him a(n) _____ because he exercised so much power during the war.

■ Illustrators and photographers accompanied Union troops during some of the war's bloodiest campaigns, leaving us an important _____ record of the horrors experienced by the soldiers on both sides of the conflict.

■ Some African Americans who have _____ from slave families have passed along dramatic stories of their ancestors' experiences.

DROUGHT LEADS TO HUNGER

■ Without enough water, plant fibers dry out and become _____. If a drought lasts for a long time, plants and crops die.

■ If too many plants die, insects have no food, and the birds and animals that _____ on insects then lose their food supply, too.

■ The threat of _____ often drives animals great distances in search of food.

■ If these animals do not _____ their hunting area, they too will starve.

A TEACHER ON A BUDGET

■ It would help our teacher a lot to have a _____ computer that she could take back and forth between school and her home.

■ She has asked businesses to donate any equipment that they no longer need. So far, more than a dozen businesses have answered her _____ with computers and monitors for our classroom.

■ It has been a very _____ way of modernizing our classroom because it has cost hardly anything at all.

Word Associations

*Circle the letter next to the word or expression that best completes the sentence or answers the question. Pay special attention to the word in **boldface**.*

1. A **dictator** is most likely
   a. to be loved
   b. to be honored
   c. to be elected
   d. to be feared

2. If a book **appeals** to you,
   a. you will probably read it
   b. it is probably very long
   c. it is probably boring
   d. you will never read it

3. Which would most likely be **condemned**?
   a. promptness
   b. cruelty
   c. generosity
   d. kindness

4. A **thrifty** person would
   a. give all of her money away
   b. never buy anything on sale
   c. count every penny
   d. leave a generous tip

5. If a rule is **abolished**,
   a. it must be obeyed
   b. it is in effect only one day
   c. it is no longer in effect
   d. it lasts forever

6. Which is a **visual** aid?
   a. a cane
   b. a set of false teeth
   c. a crutch
   d. a pair of glasses

7. If a **famine** struck,
   a. water would be scarce
   b. food would be scarce
   c. money would be scarce
   d. gasoline would be scarce

8. Which is a bird of **prey**?
   a. a canary
   b. a robin
   c. a hummingbird
   d. a hawk

9. Which might you **descend**?
   a. a ladder
   b. a lake
   c. a lily
   d. a lasso

10. If my waistline **expands**, I get
    a. taller
    b. bigger around the middle
    c. shorter
    d. smaller around the middle

11. If something is **brittle**,
    a. it breaks easily
    b. it freezes quickly
    c. it is hard to see
    d. it is easy to carry

12. Which type of house is meant to be **portable**?
    a. a 15-room mansion
    b. a house trailer
    c. a log cabin
    d. a schoolhouse

Definitions

Study the spelling, pronunciation, part of speech, and definition given for each of the words below. Write the word in the blank space in the sentence that follows. Then read the synonyms and antonyms.

1. **absurd**
(əb sûrd')

(adj.) making no sense at all, going completely against or having no reason

No one is going to believe such an _____ story!

SYNONYMS: silly, ridiculous, foolish, crazy, insane
ANTONYMS: sensible, wise, intelligent, sound

2. **avalanche**
(a' və lanch)

(n.) a large mass of snow, ice, rocks, or other material sliding or falling swiftly down a mountainside; something resembling such an event

The skiers were almost buried by an _____ that came roaring down the slope.

SYNONYMS: a landslide, flood, cascade

3. **classify**
(kla' sə fī)

(v.) to group or label in an organized way

Libraries usually _____ books by title, author, and subject.

SYNONYMS: to order, arrange, sort, catalog, pigeonhole

4. **ensure**
(en shùr')

(v.) to make sure, safe, or certain; to guarantee

The playground was designed to _____ the children's safety.

SYNONYMS: to confirm, insure
ANTONYMS: to risk, endanger

5. **navigate**
(na' və gāt)

(v.) to plan and steer the course of a vessel or vehicle; to make one's way, get around

A pilot came aboard to _____ the steamboat down the river.

SYNONYMS: to guide, pilot, operate

6. **nestle**
(ne' səl)

(v.) to settle down comfortably; to hold lovingly

When I was little, I liked to _____ in my grandmother's lap.

SYNONYMS: to cuddle, snuggle

A pilot uses charts and
instruments to **navigate**
(word 5) a helicopter.

7. **plea**
(plē)

(n.) an urgent request for help; the answer given in a law court by a
person accused of a crime
The defendant entered a _____ of not guilty.
SYNONYMS: an appeal, cry, petition, prayer

8. **principle**
(prin' sə pəl)

(n.) a basic rule or law on which others are based; a belief used to tell
right from wrong
A judge must be a person of high _____.
SYNONYMS: a standard, truth, guide, guideline, creed

9. **realistic**
(rē ə lis' tik)

(adj.) using facts and good sense to evaluate people, things, or
situations; concerned with the practical; resembling real life
The painting was so _____ that it looked like a photograph.
SYNONYMS: achievable, reasonable, sensible; true-to-life
ANTONYMS: impractical, dreamy, unrealistic, pie-in-the-sky

10. **security**
(si kyŭr' ə tē)

(n.) freedom from danger, fear, or doubt; safety
There is always heavy _____ around the White House.
SYNONYMS: protection, safekeeping, confidence, assurance
ANTONYMS: doubt, insecurity, peril

11. **selective**
(sə lek' tiv)

(adj.) very careful about choosing or using
It pays to be a very _____ shopper.
SYNONYMS: choosy, particular, picky, fussy, discriminating
ANTONYMS: unselective, careless

12. **tart**
(tärt)

(adj.) having a sharp or sour taste; sharp in manner or tone
My sister replied with a very _____ remark.
(n.) a small pie, usually filled with fruit
I had a peach _____ for dessert.
SYNONYMS: (adj.) tangy, acid; biting, cutting, harsh; (n.) a pastry
ANTONYMS: (adj.) sweet; mild, gentle

97

For each item below, choose the word whose meaning is suggested by the clue given. Then write the word in the space provided.

1. To cuddle up with something is to _____.
   a. nestle   b. navigate   c. ensure   d. classify

2. If you make sure of something, you _____ it.
   a. nestle   b. ensure   c. classify   d. navigate

3. A person of high _____ will always try to do good.
   a. avalanches   b. securities   c. pleas   d. principles

4. A fussy cat will be _____ about what it eats.
   a. absurd   b. realistic   c. selective   d. tart

5. Freedom from fear leads to a sense of _____.
   a. principle   b. plea   c. avalanche   d. security

6. To decide how to label an item is to _____ it.
   a. ensure   b. classify   c. navigate   d. nestle

7. An urgent appeal is a(n) _____ for help.
   a. plea   b. security   c. avalanche   d. principle

8. Snow tumbling down a mountain is called a(n) _____.
   a. plea   b. principle   c. avalanche   d. security

9. A statement that makes no sense is _____.
   a. realistic   b. absurd   c. selective   d. tart

10. If you judge a school on facts and evidence, you will probably get a(n) _____ sense of the place.
    a. absurd   b. selective   c. tart   d. realistic

11. To steer around obstacles is to _____ safely.
    a. ensure   b. navigate   c. classify   d. nestle

12. Lemonade without sugar tastes _____.
    a. tart   b. selective   c. realistic   d. absurd

Synonyms

*For each item below, choose the word that is most nearly the **same** in meaning as the word or phrase in **boldface**. Then write your choice on the line provided.*

1. questioned our **standards**
   a. principles   b. securities   c. pleas   d. avalanches   _____

2. a **landslide** of mail at holiday time
   a. plea   b. security   c. principle   d. avalanche   _____

3. **appeals** to save the rain forest
   a. principles   b. avalanches   c. pleas   d. securities   _____

4. **sort** the blocks by shape and color
   a. navigate   b. ensure   c. nestle   d. classify   _____

5. **cuddle** in my mother's arms
   a. classify   b. nestle   c. ensure   d. navigate   _____

6. **pilot** a tanker through the canal
   a. ensure   b. navigate   c. classify   d. nestle   _____

Antonyms

*For each item below, choose the word that is most nearly **opposite** in meaning to the word or phrase in **boldface**. Then write your choice on the line provided.*

1. to **deny** safe passage
   a. ensure   b. classify   c. navigate   d. nestle   _____

2. a **sound** excuse for being absent
   a. tart   b. absurd   c. realistic   d. selective   _____

3. show very **careless** taste
   a. selective   b. realistic   c. absurd   d. tart   _____

4. an **impractical** view of the situation
   a. absurd   b. realistic   c. selective   d. tart   _____

5. prefer **sweet** apples
   a. selective   b. realistic   c. tart   d. absurd   _____

6. felt a sense of **danger**
   a. avalanche   b. security   c. plea   d. principle   _____

Completing the Sentence

From the list of words on pages 96–97, choose the one that best completes each item below. Then write the word in the space provided. (You may have to change the word's ending.)

A DOG'S LIFE

■ Some dogs are grouped by breed or by the work that they do. Collies and komondors, for example, are labeled as herding dogs because they are both used to protect and herd sheep. Highly trained dogs that work to help people are _____ as assistance dogs.

■ Handlers of these animals have to be very _____ in choosing dogs for the demanding training. Some animals are simply not suited to the work.

■ Some dogs, such as police or guard dogs, offer _____ from crime or trespassers, helping their owners feel safer in their homes. German shepherds and Doberman pinschers are among the best known of these breeds.

■ Rescue dogs can go where humans can not or dare not go. For example, these dogs can safely _____ the ruins or rubble left by earthquakes or accidents, in search of survivors.

■ Large, strong dogs with thick fur, such as St. Bernards or huskies, are trained to rescue skiers or climbers trapped by _____.

■ Schools for these remarkable dogs make yearly _____ for money and for volunteers who will help prepare puppies for "canine careers."

CLOWNING AROUND

■ Like other schools, the Ringling Brothers Clown College is guided by a philosophy of education. At the Clown College, the first and foremost _____ is that just about anyone can be taught the art of clowning.

■ To _____ success as clowns, students must work hard to master many skills, including juggling, acrobatics, makeup design, and comedy writing.

■ Great clowns make sensible, ordinary tasks, like opening a box, somehow seem _____ and wacky.

■ Sarcastic clowns use insults and _____ comments to get laughs. Occasionally they make fun of people in the audience, but usually the clowns themselves are the butts of their own jokes.

■ In one funny routine, a clown dressed as a porcupine _____ against a cactus and called it "Mama."

■ The cactus looked quite _____ and lifelike from a distance, but on closer inspection it proved to be made of rubber.

Word Associations

*Circle the letter next to the word or expression that best completes the sentence or answers the question. Pay special attention to the word in **boldface.***

1. Which would be an **absurd** gift for a two-year-old?
   a. a toy drum
   b. a beach ball
   c. a dinosaur puppet
   d. a real sports car

2. Where might you see an **avalanche**?
   a. on the ocean
   b. in the mountains
   c. in a desert
   d. in a suburb

3. You *cannot* be **classified** as
   a. a mammal
   b. a student
   c. a human being
   d. a plant

4. Which is a **plea**?
   a. "Thank you!"
   b. "That's an order!"
   c. "I forgot my lunch."
   d. "Not guilty, your honor."

5. Athletes with strong **principles**
   a. play by the rules
   b. fight with the coach
   c. hold out for more money
   d. skip practice

6. Studying hard will help **ensure**
   a. good manners
   b. good looks
   c. good weather
   d. good grades

7. Which will probably be **tart**?
   a. honey
   b. butterscotch pudding
   c. lemon juice
   d. blueberry pie

8. If a kitten **nestles**
   a. it scratches and howls
   b. it cuddles and purrs
   c. it chases a mouse
   d. it laps up milk

9. A movie about a **realistic** situation might be titled
   a. "I Married an Alligator!"
   b. "The Magic Eggplant"
   c. "Forest Fire!"
   d. "Martian Dance Party"

10. A sense of **security** makes you feel
    a. upset
    b. nervous
    c. safe
    d. lucky

11. A **selective** person might be called
    a. "Pokey Polly"
    b. "Picky Peter"
    c. "Wacky William"
    d. "Forgetful Fran"

12. Which is easiest to **navigate**?
    a. a bicycle
    b. a hot air balloon
    c. a bucking bronco
    d. a sailboat

Definitions

Study the spelling, pronunciation, part of speech, and definition given for each of the words below. Write the word in the blank space in the sentence that follows. Then read the synonyms and antonyms.

1. **abuse**
   (*n.*, ə byüs′;
   v., ə byüz′)

   (n.) improper, wrong, or cruel treatment; insulting language
   The _____ of power is a danger in any government.

   (v.) to put to bad use; to hurt or damage by treating badly
   If you _____ your privileges, they may be taken away.

   SYNONYMS: (n.) misuse, mistreatment; (v.) to harm, injure; to insult
   ANTONYMS: (n.) care, support; (v.) to cherish, honor, praise

2. **appliance**
   (ə plī′ əns)

   (n.) a machine or tool used to do a household job
   It seemed an awfully big claim for such a little _____.

   SYNONYMS: a device, utensil, contraption, gadget

3. **confirm**
   (kən fûrm′)

   (v.) to agree or prove that something is true; to make sure, remove any doubt
   The press secretary refused to _____ the report.

   SYNONYMS: to verify, support, assure; to check
   ANTONYMS: to deny, disprove; to cancel

4. **daze**
   (dāz)

   (v.) to stun or confuse
   Some predators _____ their prey with a blow to the head.

   (n.) a state of confusion
   When I heard that I had won the prize, I walked around in a

   _____.

   SYNONYMS: (v.) to numb, shock, astound, baffle, bewilder; (n.) a trance, stupor

5. **flimsy**
   (flim′ zē)

   (adj.) not strong or solid; poorly made; not convincing
   I don't think my teacher believed my _____ excuse for not doing my homework.

   SYNONYMS: thin, light, weak, rickety, feeble; shabby, shoddy
   ANTONYMS: strong, sturdy, sound; convincing

6. **gauge**
   (gāj)

   (n.) a standard measure used to tell size, thickness, and so on; an instrument used to measure
   Weather scientists use a _____ to measure rainfall.

   (v.) to measure; to estimate
   The cat seemed to _____ the distance before jumping onto the windowsill.

   SYNONYMS: (n.) a scale, rule, yardstick; (v.) to judge, assess; to guess

Ballerinas are taught to **rotate** (word 11)
while balancing on one toe in order
to perform pirouettes, or spins.

7. **migrant**
(mī′ grənt)

(n.) an animal or person that moves from one region to another as the seasons change; a farmworker who moves seasonally to pick different crops
  We passed a field full of _____ picking berries.
SYNONYMS: a traveler, nomad, drifter

8. **neutral**
(nü′ trəl)

(adj.) not taking any side in a disagreement or war; in-between, lacking distinction; not in gear
  Switzerland remained _____ through both World Wars I and II.
SYNONYMS: uninvolved, uncommitted, impartial, open-minded; indefinite, vague
ANTONYMS: involved, committed, opinionated, heated; bold

9. **pitiless**
(pi′ ti ləs)

(adj.) showing no sorrow or regret for another's suffering or troubles
  The audience booed the _____ villain.
SYNONYMS: cold, merciless, heartless, unsparing, cruel
ANTONYMS: kindhearted, merciful, sympathetic

10. **presentable**
(pri zen′ tə bəl)

(adj.) fit to be seen or inspected
  My parents insisted that I wear _____ clothing.
SYNONYMS: suitable, proper, respectable, passable
ANTONYMS: shabby, improper, unfit, unacceptable

11. **rotate**
(rō′ tāt)

(v.) to turn around a central point; to alternate
  Do you know how long it takes Earth to _____ once?
SYNONYMS: to circle, twirl, spin; to change, switch

12. **shred**
(shred)

(n.) a thin strip; a tiny piece or amount
  Not a _____ of evidence was found.
(v.) to cut or tear into thin strips or small pieces; to rip up
  The secretary was asked to _____ the document.
SYNONYMS: (n.) a scrap, tatter, bit, fragment
ANTONYMS: (n.) a whole; (v.) to fix, mend, repair

103

Match the Meaning

For each item below, choose the word whose meaning is suggested by the clue given. Then write the word in the space provided.

1. To use something in a way that brings harm to yourself or others is to _____ it.
   a. gauge   b. rotate   c. daze   d. abuse

2. If you have been stunned, you might be in a(n) _____.
   a. gauge   b. daze   c. appliance   d. shred

3. To tear something to pieces is to _____ it.
   a. abuse   b. daze   c. shred   d. rotate

4. A _____ foe would not show mercy.
   a. flimsy   b. presentable   c. pitiless   d. neutral

5. Not to take sides is to remain _____.
   a. pitiless   b. presentable   c. flimsy   d. neutral

6. To prove something is to _____ it.
   a. daze   b. confirm   c. rotate   d. gauge

7. People or animals that move to different regions as the seasons change are called _____.
   a. migrants   b. gauges   c. appliances   d. shreds

8. Blenders and can openers are kitchen _____.
   a. migrants   b. shreds   c. appliances   d. gauges

9. Something poorly made is said to be _____.
   a. presentable   b. flimsy   c. pitiless   d. neutral

10. A room fit to be inspected is _____.
    a. flimsy   b. pitiless   c. neutral   d. presentable

11. To alternate chores is to _____ them.
    a. shred   b. rotate   c. abuse   d. gauge

12. You would use a _____ to measure something.
    a. gauge   b. shred   c. daze   d. migrant

1. an electrical **device** for cleaning rugs
   a. shred   b. migrant   c. gauge   d. appliance   _____

2. left behind by the **drifters**
   a. shreds   b. abuses   c. migrants   d. gauges   _____

3. wore a **respectable** outfit for the class picture
   a. presentable   b. flimsy   c. neutral   d. pitiless   _____

4. **numbed** by the terrible news
   a. gauged   b. dazed   c. rotated   d. confirmed   _____

5. **assess** the value of the coin collection
   a. shred   b. gauge   c. abuse   d. rotate   _____

6. **twirl** the plant to face the sun
   a. confirm   b. gauge   c. daze   d. rotate   _____

Antonyms For each item below, choose the word that is most nearly **opposite** in meaning to the word or phrase in **boldface**. Then write your choice on the line provided.

1. **mend** the old pillowcase
   a. shred   b. confirm   c. rotate   d. gauge   _____

2. **sturdy** shoes
   a. neutral   b. flimsy   c. presentable   d. pitiless   _____

3. reported their **kindhearted** treatment
   a. neutral   b. flimsy   c. presentable   d. pitiless   _____

4. refused to **deny** the rumor
   a. gauge   b. rotate   c. confirm   d. classify   _____

5. painted in **bold** colors
   a. flimsy   b. neutral   c. presentable   d. pitiless   _____

6. fans who **praise** the umpires
   a. rotate   b. gauge   c. abuse   d. daze   _____

Completing the Sentence

From the list of words on pages 102–103, choose the one that best completes each item below. Then write the word in the space provided. (You may have to change the word's ending.)

■ One of the most common of household _____, the electric toaster, was first introduced to American kitchens in 1910.

■ Early models toasted only one side of the bread at a time. In order to toast both sides, you had to _____ the slice of bread yourself.

■ These toasters did not have self-timers, either. If you didn't pay careful attention, your toast might not look very _____. And if it had turned to ashes, it might not even be fit to eat!

■ It is estimated that in the United States there are today about half a million _____ who follow the harvest each year in search of work at fruit and vegetable farms.

■ Unfortunately, these workers are often _____ by harsh bosses who pay too little and demand too much. To make matters worse, working and living conditions are often unsafe and unsanitary.

■ Bending over for hours under a hot sun to harvest crops can leave these workers feeling _____ by the end of a long day in the fields.

■ The _____ sun beats down on the workers, offering no mercy to man, woman, or child.

■ Some farmworkers are so poor that they barely get enough to eat, and their old, tattered clothes hang in _____.

■ Rather than stay _____ about the problems that seasonal farmworkers face, some activists are taking up their cause by fighting for improved legal and civil rights.

■ When our car came sputtering to a stop on a dark and lonely country road, I was almost afraid to look at the fuel _____.

■ But when I did, a quick glance was enough to _____ the worst: The car had run out of gas, just as I suspected.

■ We had to walk two miles to a gas station, with nothing more to protect us from the rain than our _____ jackets. When we got back to the car with a container of fuel, we were completely soaked and shivering with cold.

Word Associations

*Circle the letter next to the word or expression that best completes the sentence or answers the question. Pay special attention to the word in **boldface**.*

1. A **flimsy** toy will probably
   a. cost lots of money
   b. break much too soon
   c. be very popular
   d. come in many colors

2. To **confirm** a fact for a social studies report, you might
   a. check an encyclopedia
   b. read a science-fiction novel
   c. copy the paper neatly
   d. call your doctor

3. If you're in a **daze**, you may
   a. yell at your friends
   b. remember to water the plants
   c. not notice the time
   d. turn the calendar page

4. Birds that are **migrants** probably
   a. have blue feathers
   b. lay only one egg at a time
   c. eat fruits and vegetables
   d. travel in the spring and fall

5. Which is known for **rotating**?
   a. a teddy bear
   b. a top
   c. a book
   d. a sandwich

6. A **neutral** nation would not be
   a in debt
   b. an island
   c. at war
   d. at peace

7. Which is easiest to **shred**?
   a. a loaf of bread
   b. a brass ring
   c. a suit of armor
   d. a spike

8. A piano that has been **abused**
   a. would sound better
   b. might be out of tune
   c. would increase in value
   d. might be hard to move

9. A **pitiless** person would make others
   a. feel unloved
   b. feel unfamiliar
   c. feel at ease
   d. feel proud

10. Which might you need to **gauge**?
    a. the distance from Earth to the moon
    b. a friend's height
    c. the amount of gold in Fort Knox
    d. the width of a cat's whisker

11. To make your room more **presentable**, you might
    a. feed your hamster
    b. put away your clothes and toys
    c. open the window
    d. lock the door

12. Which is an **appliance**?
    a. a box of laundry detergent
    b. a laundry room
    c. a laundry basket
    d. a washing machine

REVIEW UNITS 9–12

For vocabulary games and activities, visit **www.sadlier-oxford.com**.

Selecting Word Meanings

*For each of the following items, circle the choice that is most nearly the **same** in meaning as the word in **boldface**.*

1. check the latest opinion **poll**
   - a. speech
   - b. survey
   - c. software
   - d. timetable

2. learn **thrifty** habits
   - a. money-saving
   - b. childish
   - c. wasteful
   - d. nervous

3. **rotate** the schedule
   - a. write
   - b. memorize
   - c. switch
   - d. stick to

4. **identical** patterns
   - a. matching
   - b. complicated
   - c. unusual
   - d. colorful

5. **neutral** reporting
   - a. opinionated
   - b. careless
   - c. realistic
   - d. unbiased

6. **classify** the types of insects
   - a. read about
   - b. preserve
   - c. catalog
   - d. photograph

7. **humiliated** the defending champions
   - a. congratulated
   - b. embarrassed
   - c. cheered for
   - d. disliked

8. **confirm** the dental appointment
   - a. make sure of
   - b. reschedule
   - c. cancel
   - d. fear

9. studied the **principles** of multiplication
   - a. questions
   - b. challenges
   - c. rules
   - d. theories

10. a **brisk** early morning swim
    - a. slow
    - b. relaxing
    - c. exhausting
    - d. energetic

11. **expand** the search
    - a. join
    - b. widen
    - c. end
    - d. begin

12. **considerate** neighbors
    - a. friendly
    - b. noisy
    - c. thoughtful
    - d. sneaky

Spelling

For each item below, study the **boldface** word in which there is a blank. If a letter is missing, fill in the blank to make a correctly spelled word. If the word is already spelled correctly, leave the blank empty.

1. numbers on a **ga__uge**

2. an **avalanch__** of bills

3. **so__the** my aching head

4. a desperate **ple__a**

5. a labor-saving **ap__liance**

6. lost in a **da__ze**

7. **condem__** the attack

8. **des__end** a staircase

9. **migr__nt** whales

10. an **abs__rd** suggestion

11. a **present__ble** appearance

12. fought against the **dictat__r**

Antonyms

For each of the following items, circle the choice that is most nearly the **opposite** in meaning to the word in **boldface** in the introductory phrase.

1. **confirmed** my fears
   a. explained   b. disproved   c. ignored   d. supported

2. **brittle** tree branches
   a. stiff   b. slender   c. bendable   d. thick

3. **shred** the old photograph
   a. mend   b. tear up   c. throw away   d. lose

4. **tart** fruits
   a. tangy   b. ripe   c. frozen   d. sweet

5. speak out against **abuse**
   a. kindness   b. mistreatment   c. knowledge   d. humor

6. a **portable** stage
   a. fixed   b. movable   c. small   d. bare

7. a **flimsy** explanation
   a. lengthy   b. weak   c. complicated   d. convincing

8. **improper** way of doing things
   a. wrong   b. awkward   c. correct   d. simple

*Read the following passage in which some of the words you have studied appear in **boldface**. Then answer the questions on page 111.*

Making Sense of a Scientific Survey

The U.S. Census Bureau takes official surveys to gather data on our population. The formal count is called a *census*. Business leaders, educators, and politicians use the data to get a **realistic** picture of the people they serve and the needs of the community.

Scientists also use census data. Can you imagine why? Scientists study plant and animal populations for many reasons. Scientists might track animal populations to learn how animals and humans can live together safely. They might study specific fish populations in a pond to get information about water pollution. Or they might count the members of an endangered species to **confirm** that the animals need ongoing protection.

Government census workers gather data in person and by mail. But scientists must find unique ways to count the plants or animals in a given area. To **estimate** the population of free-tailed bats in Carlsbad Cavern, the largest cave in New Mexico, scientists made use of technology. They set up video cameras outside the entrance of the cave, which houses a large number of bats. The scientists taped the bats flying out of the cave. Later, they counted the bats in each frame of the video.

Free-tailed bats emerging from caves to hunt

Scientists sometimes use just their eyes to take a census. This **visual** method works best when the plants or animals are large in size and small in number. For example, to count the maple trees on a farm in Vermont, scientists can simply use their eyes. A more complex method would be needed to determine the number of small animals, such as field mice, in the same **vicinity**.

Fill in the circle next to the choice that best completes the sentence or answers the question.

1. What is the main idea of this article?
   - (a) The U.S. Census Bureau gathers useful population data.
   - (b) Like the government, scientists gather and use census data.
   - (c) Carlsbad, New Mexico, is an interesting place to visit.
   - (d) Scientists use their eyes to count many living things.

2. The meaning of **realistic** is
   - (a) true-to-life
   - (b) scientific
   - (c) superb
   - (d) strict

3. Another word for **confirm** is
   - (a) question
   - (b) disprove
   - (c) suggest
   - (d) verify

4. Scientists might investigate plant and animal populations
   - (a) to learn about polluted cities
   - (b) to educate American voters
   - (c) to see if a species is endangered
   - (d) to test new voting machines

5. In this passage, **estimate** means
   - (a) calculation
   - (b) opinion
   - (c) figure
   - (d) praise

6. The method for counting bats described in this passage involves
   - (a) using just eyes
   - (b) gathering data by mail
   - (c) questioning neighbors
   - (d) videotaping a cave entrance

7. **Visual** means having to do with
   - (a) sound or hearing
   - (b) sight or seeing
   - (c) feel or touching
   - (d) scent or smelling

8. Another word for **vicinity** is
   - (a) tally
   - (b) state
   - (c) area
   - (d) laboratory

9. This article was written to inform people of
   - (a) how scientists gather and use data
   - (b) an estimation technique
   - (c) the need for scientific data
   - (d) a new plant species

10. Which is the most likely topic for the next paragraph in the article?
    - (a) when the first census was taken
    - (b) the number of farms in Vermont
    - (c) the way to take a census of small forest animals
    - (d) other wildlife in Carlsbad

Grammar in Context

An **adjective** is a word that describes a noun. It tells what the person, place, or thing is like.

Use the correct form of an adjective when you compare.

> You usually add **er** to an adjective to compare two people, places, or things.
>
> Ice Cave is **larger** than Lava Cave.
>
> You usually add **est** to an adjective to compare three or more people, places, or things.
>
> Carlsbad Caverns is the **largest** cave in New Mexico.

For adjectives ending in **e**, drop the **e** before adding **er** or **est**.

*Use the correct form of the adjective in **boldface** to complete the sentence. Then write the sentence on the line.*

1. A healthy branch is (**strong**) than a dry and brittle twig. ⎯⎯⎯⎯⎯⎯⎯⎯⎯⎯

⎯⎯⎯⎯⎯⎯⎯⎯⎯⎯⎯⎯⎯⎯⎯⎯⎯⎯⎯⎯⎯⎯⎯⎯⎯⎯⎯⎯⎯⎯⎯⎯⎯⎯⎯⎯⎯⎯

2. The bats prey upon the (**small**) insects of all. ⎯⎯⎯⎯⎯⎯⎯⎯⎯⎯⎯⎯

⎯⎯⎯⎯⎯⎯⎯⎯⎯⎯⎯⎯⎯⎯⎯⎯⎯⎯⎯⎯⎯⎯⎯⎯⎯⎯⎯⎯⎯⎯⎯⎯⎯⎯⎯⎯⎯⎯

3. Bats can navigate even on the (**dark**) nights. ⎯⎯⎯⎯⎯⎯⎯⎯⎯⎯⎯⎯⎯

⎯⎯⎯⎯⎯⎯⎯⎯⎯⎯⎯⎯⎯⎯⎯⎯⎯⎯⎯⎯⎯⎯⎯⎯⎯⎯⎯⎯⎯⎯⎯⎯⎯⎯⎯⎯⎯⎯

4. The visitors descend into the (**deep**) cave in New Mexico. ⎯⎯⎯⎯⎯⎯⎯

⎯⎯⎯⎯⎯⎯⎯⎯⎯⎯⎯⎯⎯⎯⎯⎯⎯⎯⎯⎯⎯⎯⎯⎯⎯⎯⎯⎯⎯⎯⎯⎯⎯⎯⎯⎯⎯⎯

5. The security guard directs us to the (**close**) exit. ⎯⎯⎯⎯⎯⎯⎯⎯⎯⎯

⎯⎯⎯⎯⎯⎯⎯⎯⎯⎯⎯⎯⎯⎯⎯⎯⎯⎯⎯⎯⎯⎯⎯⎯⎯⎯⎯⎯⎯⎯⎯⎯⎯⎯⎯⎯⎯⎯

6. The guard's jacket is (**warm**) than my flimsy sweater. ⎯⎯⎯⎯⎯⎯⎯⎯

⎯⎯⎯⎯⎯⎯⎯⎯⎯⎯⎯⎯⎯⎯⎯⎯⎯⎯⎯⎯⎯⎯⎯⎯⎯⎯⎯⎯⎯⎯⎯⎯⎯⎯⎯⎯⎯⎯

Completing the Idea

*Complete each sentence so that it makes sense. Pay attention to the word in **boldface**.*

1. I take **brisk** walks in the morning because _____.

2. The twins are nearly **identical**, except that _____.

3. In a **poll** about the election, I was asked _____.

4. A good way to **soothe** sore feet is to _____.

5. A folding table is **portable** because _____.

6. We could **expand** the team by _____.

7. Because of the **famine**, many people _____.

8. To **ensure** that I wake up on time, I will _____.

9. I like to **classify** my books by _____.

10. If I **shred** the pages in my diary, then _____.

11. I have a sense of **security** knowing that _____.

12. For a **tart** taste, I recommend _____.

13. One household **appliance** I cannot live without is _____.

14. I was in a **daze** when I heard that _____.

15. To look more **presentable**, please _____.

Write Your Own

*Choose a word from Units 9–12. Write a sentence using the word.
If your sentence contains an adjective, be sure you used the correct
form of the adjective.*

_____

_____

*The words in **boldface** in the sentences below are related to words introduced in Units 9–12. For example, the nouns* confirmation *and* navigation *in item 1 are related to the verbs* confirm *(Unit 12) and* navigate *(Unit 11). Based on your understanding of the unit words that follow, circle the related word in **boldface** that best completes each sentence.*

absurd	abuse	classify	condemn	confirm
considerate	descend	displace	estimate	expand
flimsy	humiliate	improper	migrant	navigate
neutral	poll	portable	presentable	rotate

1. The U.S. Senate is responsible for the (**confirmation/navigation**) of the President's nominees for ambassadorships.

2. Queen Elizabeth II of England is a direct (**classification/descendant**) of Queen Victoria.

3. A figure skater who successfully performs a quadruple jump completes four (**rotations/considerations**) in the air.

4. A public official who takes a bribe is guilty of (**impropriety/absurdity**).

5. Scientists use photographs of the one-of-a-kind markings on the tail fins of humpback whales as one tool in tracking the (**migration/expansion**) of these marine mammals.

6. During an election campaign, (**pollsters/abusers**) question voters about which candidates they prefer.

7. One of the advantages of a personal stereo is its (**presentability/ portability**).

8. In math we learn that(**displacement/estimation**) can sometimes help us solve problems.

9. While a trial is in progress, the judge repeatedly instructs the jury to maintain its (**neutrality/flimsiness**) until all the testimony and evidence have been presented.

10. The policitian's insensitive remarks received public (**humiliation/ condemnation**).

Use the clues below to complete the crossword puzzle.
(All of the answers are words from Units 9–12.)

Down

1. to move aside
3.
6. do away with completely
8. cuddle
10. poorly made

Across

2. neighborhood
4. tear to bits
5. lifelike
7. widespread hunger
9. collapse or ruin
11. without mercy
12. predator's victim

Definitions

Study the spelling, pronunciation, part of speech, and definition given for each of the words below. Write the word in the blank space in the sentence that follows. Then read the synonyms and antonyms.

1. **achievement**
   (ə chēv′ mənt)

   (n.) something done successfully; something gained by working or trying hard
   > *A perfect report card is quite an _____.*

   SYNONYMS: an accomplishment, feat, triumph
   ANTONYMS: a defeat, failure, setback

2. **acquire**
   (ə kwīr′)

   (v.) to get as one's own
   > *When did you _____ the ability to speak French so well?*

   SYNONYMS: to obtain, gain, earn
   ANTONYMS: to lose, give up, surrender

3. **debate**
   (di bāt′)

   (n.) a discussion of reasons for and against something
   > *The town council held a _____ on building a new library.*

   (v.) to discuss reasons for and against something; to think about carefully before deciding
   > *What issue would you like to _____?*

   SYNONYMS: (n.) an argument, dispute; (v.) to discuss, consider
   ANTONYMS: (n.) an agreement; (v.) to agree (with)

4. **exhibit**
   (ig zi′ bət)

   (v.) to show clearly; to put on display
   > *You _____ great talent in gymnastics.*

   (n.) something shown to the public
   > *We went to the diamond _____ at the science museum.*

   SYNONYMS: (v.) to present, reveal; (n.) a display, exhibition
   ANTONYMS: (v.) to hide, conceal, cover up

5. **foe**
   (fō)

   (n.) one who hates or tries to harm another; an enemy
   > *Identify yourself: Are you friend or _____?*

   SYNONYMS: an opponent, rival
   ANTONYMS: a friend, ally, comrade, buddy

6. **latter**
   (la′ tər)

   (adj.) closer to the end; relating to the second of two things discussed
   > *The first part of the movie is good, but the _____ part drags on too long.*

   SYNONYMS: last, later, end, final
   ANTONYMS: former, first, earlier, beginning

Some people who make computer parts have to wear special clothing to keep their work area completely **sanitary** (word 10).

7. **massacre**
   (ma' si kər)

(n.) the cruel killing of many people or animals
The village was the site of a bloody _____.

(v.) to kill many people or animals in a cruel way
The barbarians planned to _____ *their rivals.*

SYNONYMS: (n.) a slaughter; (v.) to butcher, slaughter

8. **monotonous**
   (mə nä' tən əs)

(adj.) dull as a result of not changing in any way
Shelling peas is a _____ *chore.*

SYNONYMS: boring, uninteresting, tiresome
ANTONYMS: varied, lively, exciting

9. **preserve**
   (pri zûrv')

(v.) to keep safe from injury or ruin; to keep food from spoiling
I signed a petition to _____ *the wetlands.*

(n.) an area set aside for the protection of wildlife
Wild animals roam freely in the nature _____.

SYNONYMS: (v.) to save, protect, conserve; (n.) a refuge, sanctuary
ANTONYMS: (v.) to waste, destroy, misuse

10. **sanitary**
    (sa' nə ter ē)

(adj.) having to do with health; free of dirt and germs
A health inspector checks _____ *conditions in a restaurant.*

SYNONYMS: clean, pure, sterile, hygienic
ANTONYMS: dirty, filthy, contaminated, unhealthy

11. **sprawl**
    (sprôl)

(v.) to lie or sit with arms and legs spread out; to spread out in a disorderly way
Some nights I _____ *in front of the TV set.*

SYNONYMS: to lounge, slouch, relax, stretch, extend

12. **widespread**
    (wīd' spred')

(adj.) happening in many places or to many people; fully open
Interest in the lives of movie stars is _____.

SYNONYMS: far-reaching, vast, common
ANTONYMS: limited, rare, unusual, uncommon

Match the Meaning

For each item below, choose the word whose meaning is suggested by the clue given. Then write the word in the space provided.

1. A display of paintings or other objects is a(n) _____.
   a. debate   b. exhibit   c. massacre   d. preserve

2. A belief that is held by many people is _____.
   a. latter   b. monotonous   c. widespread   d. sanitary

3. When you buy property, you _____ it.
   a. massacre   b. sprawl   c. debate   d. acquire

4. People who hate one another are _____.
   a. achievements   b. foes   c. debates   d. exhibits

5. The cruel killing of many innocent people is a(n) _____.
   a. massacre   b. exhibit   c. achievement   d. foe

6. Something that is free of germs is _____.
   a. widespread   b. monotonous   c. latter   d. sanitary

7. To consider the pros and cons of an issue is to _____ it.
   a. debate   b. exhibit   c. preserve   d. acquire

8. A bird sanctuary is an example of a wildlife _____.
   a. debate   b. massacre   c. preserve   d. foe

9. The second of two events is the _____ one.
   a. monotonous   b. latter   c. sanitary   d. widespread

10. Landing on the moon is an example of a(n) _____.
    a. foe   b. achievement   c. massacre   d. preserve

11. Something that is done over and over in the same way is _____.
    a. latter   b. widespread   c. sanitary   d. monotonous

12. To lie on the floor with your arms and legs spread out is to _____.
    a. exhibit   b. preserve   c. sprawl   d. acquire

*For each item below, choose the word that is most nearly the **same** in meaning as the word or phrase in **boldface**. Then write your choice on the line provided.*

1. a worthy **opponent**
   a. preserve b. exhibit c. foe   d. debate   _____

2. **slaughter** the newborn harp seals
   a. preserve b. exhibit c. acquire d. massacre _____

3. the **boring** refrain of "tra-la-la"
   a. latter   b. sanitary c. widespread d. monotonous _____

4. **consider** going by train or by car
   a. sprawl b. debate c. acquire d. massacre _____

5. my proudest **accomplishment**
   a. preserve b. exhibit c. foe   d. achievement _____

6. **lounge** on the couch
   a. exhibit b. preserve c. sprawl d. massacre _____

*For each item below, choose the word that is most nearly **opposite** in meaning to the word or phrase in **boldface**. Then write your choice on the line provided.*

1. **conceal** your surprise
   a. exhibit b. sprawl c. massacre d. preserve _____

2. the **first** part of our vacation
   a. widespread b. latter c. monotonous d. sanitary _____

3. **lose** millions of dollars
   a. debate b. sprawl c. massacre d. acquire _____

4. **limited** appeal among children
   a. sanitary b. monotonous c. latter d. widespread _____

5. **destroy** the town records
   a. massacre b. exhibit c. preserve d. sprawl _____

6. found **unhealthy** living conditions
   a. latter   b. sanitary c. widespread d. monotonous _____

Completing the Sentence

From the list of words on pages 116–117, choose the one that best completes each item below. Write the word in the space provided. (You may have to change the word's ending.)

YOU CAN'T WIN THEM ALL

■ The current events club had to decide whether to _____ hunters' rights or the child helmet law.

■ We chose the child helmet law, the _____ issue, because it was more relevant to students our age.

■ The members of our team gave such _____ speeches in favor of the law that the other team won, although their arguments were more emotional than fact-filled.

WHAT HAPPENED IN RWANDA

■ In 1994 a brutal _____ took place in Rwanda, a country in Central Africa. Hundreds of thousands of people were injured or killed.

■ The major _____ were the Hutu and Tutsi peoples.

■ In overcrowded refugee camps, _____ conditions were dangerously poor. Clean water, food, and medicines were in short supply.

■ Rescue workers found entire families _____ on the ground. Many of these people were dying of starvation and disease.

"FOUR SCORE AND SEVEN YEARS AGO. . ."

■ Many historians consider Abraham Lincoln's Gettysburg Address to be the greatest _____ in public speaking this nation has produced.

■ The fame of this brief speech is so _____ that most Americans—and even many from other nations—know the opening of it by heart.

■ The Library of Congress _____ a copy of the speech, written in Lincoln's own hand. Only four other copies in his handwriting are still in existence.

■ At the library the manuscript is carefully _____ as a national historical treasure.

■ Sometimes the document travels to Pennsylvania for _____ in connection with special events at the actual site of the battle. The battlefield became a national park in 1895.

*Circle the letter next to the word or expression that best completes the sentence or answers the question. Pay special attention to the word in **boldface.***

1. A cafeteria that is **sanitary** has
   a. good main dishes
   b. overflowing trash bins
   c. safely prepared food
   d. high-priced lunches

2. The **latter** part of December includes
   a. the first day of the month
   b. the last week of the month
   c. four Sundays
   d. New Year's Day

3. If my neighbor is my **foe,** we
   a. share a driveway
   b. do not get along
   c. live in the country
   d. feed each other's pets

4. Witnesses to a **massacre** probably feel
   a. horrified
   b. cheerful
   c. hungry
   d. relaxed

5. A **monotonous** speaker might
   a. win an award for public speaking
   b. wake up the neighborhood
   c. give speech lessons
   d. put a listener to sleep

6. A swimmer who is honored for his or her **achievements** might
   a. go waterskiing
   b. get a sunburn
   c. get a trophy
   d. go to an aquarium

7. Which of these has been **preserved**?
   a. apples on a tree
   b. berries on a vine
   c. fresh peach pie
   d. canned pears

8. Which might be included in an **exhibit** of students' work?
   a. paintings by famous artists
   b. science fair projects
   c. parents and teachers
   d. rulers and erasers

9. One way to **acquire** a rare stamp is to
   a. mail a letter
   b. read a book about collecting stamps
   c. buy one from a catalog
   d. pay extra postage

10. A participant in a **debate** should
    a. defend his or her point of view
    b. try not to say anything
    c. never argue with an opponent
    d. join the football team

11. Which of these is **widespread**?
    a. an opinion held by a few friends
    b. a belief that the earth is flat
    c. an interest in fruitflies
    d. a disease that infects many people

12. I might **sprawl** on the couch to
    a. relax
    b. wake up
    c. move furniture
    d. exercise

Definitions

Study the spelling, pronunciation, part of speech, and definition given for each of the words below. Write the word in the blank space in the sentence that follows. Then read the synonyms and antonyms.

1. **alibi**
   (a' lə bī)

   (n.) a claim of having been elsewhere when a crime was committed; a reason given to explain something
   Can anyone confirm your _____?
   SYNONYMS: an excuse, explanation, story, defense

2. **confederate**
   (kən fe' də rət)

   (adj.) joined with others for a common purpose
   Seven sheikdoms are _____ states in the United Arab Emirates.

   (n.) a person, state, or country that joins with another for a common purpose; a partner in crime
   Some of our wartime allies are still our _____ in peacekeeping organizations.
   SYNONYMS: (adj.) united, allied, combined; (n.) an ally, accomplice
   ANTONYMS: (adj.) divided, separated; (n.) a foe, enemy

3. **discharge**
   (v., dis chärj';
   n., dis' chärj)

   (v.) to let go; to unload cargo or passengers; to fire off; to give off
   Did the hospital _____ the patient?

   (n.) a release or letting go; a firing off; a giving off; something given off
   A search of the records showed that the army gave the soldier an honorable _____.
   SYNONYMS: (v.) to release, dismiss, shoot; (n.) a dismissal
   ANTONYMS: (v.) to detain, imprison; to hire, appoint; to load; to absorb

4. **economical**
   (e kə nä' mi kəl)

   (adj.) careful about spending money or using resources
   An _____ shopper waits for sales and always looks for a bargain.
   SYNONYMS: thrifty, frugal, saving
   ANTONYMS: extravagant, wasteful

5. **frank**
   (fraŋk)

   (adj.) honest in expressing thoughts and feelings
   Don't be offended if I am _____ with you.
   SYNONYMS: direct, blunt, straightforward, truthful
   ANTONYMS: secretive, insincere, dishonest

6. **modify**
   (mä' də fī)

   (v.) to change somewhat
   A good cook knows how to _____ a recipe if one or two of the ingredients are not available.
   SYNONYMS: to adjust, alter, adapt, vary, revise

7. **mutiny**
(myü′ tən ē)

(n.) an open rebellion against authority
  The Boston Tea Party was an act of _____.
(v.) to rebel against those in charge
  The captain's cruelty led the crew to _____.
SYNONYMS: (n.) a revolt, uprising, riot; (v.) to revolt, rise up
ANTONYMS: (n.) to support, obey

8. **negative**
(ne′ gə tiv)

(adj.) saying "no"; not positive or helpful; less than zero; having the same electric charge as an electron
  The reply to my question was _____.
(n.) an expression that says "no"; a photographic image in which light and dark areas are reversed
  "I can't" is an example of a _____.
SYNONYMS: (adj.) bad, unfavorable
ANTONYMS: (adj.) positive, helpful, good, favorable

9. **pursue**
(pər sü′)

(v.) to chase in order to catch; to strive to achieve; to carry out
  During a hunt the dogs _____ *a hare.*
SYNONYMS: to follow, hunt, run after, aim for, work for
ANTONYMS: to run away, take off, flee, bolt

10. **reign**
(rān)

(n.) the power or rule of a monarch; a monarch's period of rule
  England prospered under the _____ *of Queen Anne.*
(v.) to rule as a monarch; to be widespread
  During the 1920s, prosperity _____.
SYNONYMS: (n.) the regime, control; (v.) to govern, command

11. **singular**
(siŋ′ gyə lər)

(adj.) referring to one person or thing only; out of the ordinary
  The show was a _____ *success.*
(n.) the form of a word that is used to refer to one person or thing
  "Mouse" is the _____ *of "mice."*
SYNONYMS: (adj.) exceptional, unusual
ANTONYMS: (adj.) plural; (n.) a plural

12. **swindle**
(swin′ dəl)

(v.) to cheat out of money or property
  A dishonest shopkeeper tried to _____ *me.*
(n.) a scheme for cheating someone
  The fraud squad uncovered the _____.
SYNONYMS: (v.) to deceive, trick, gyp, con; (n.) a scam, fraud, hoax, racket

123

Match the Meaning

For each item below, choose the word whose meaning is suggested by the clue given. Then write the word in the space provided.

1. To rebel against commanding officers is to _____.
   a. discharge   b. swindle   c. modify   d. mutiny

2. To exercise the powers of a king or queen is to _____.
   a. reign   b. pursue   c. mutiny   d. modify

3. A scheme for cheating people is a _____.
   a. negative   b. discharge   c. swindle   d. confederate

4. A claim of being elsewhere during a crime is a(n) _____.
   a. alibi   b. mutiny   c. discharge   d. reign

5. When you change plans slightly, you _____ them.
   a. modify   b. discharge   c. swindle   d. pursue

6. A person who freely expresses his or her opinion is _____.
   a. confederate   b. economical   c. negative   d. frank

7. When you fire a gun, you _____ it.
   a. swindle   b. discharge   c. pursue   d. modify

8. A person who is careful about spending money is _____.
   a. frank   b. negative   c. economical   d. singular

9. A person who makes a suggestion that is not helpful is being _____.
   a. economical   b. negative   c. frank   d. singular

10. A willing accomplice to a robbery is a(n) _____ of the thief.
    a. confederate   b. alibi   c. discharge   d. mutiny

11. The anniversary celebration was the _____ event of the year.
    a. frank   b. singular   c. confederate   d. economical

12. When you keep trying to achieve a goal, you _____ it.
    a. modify   b. discharge   c. pursue   d. swindle

Synonyms

*For each item below, choose the word that is most nearly the **same** in meaning as the word or phrase in **boldface**. Then write your choice on the line provided.*

1. a **blunt** answer to your question
   a. frank   b. negative   c. singular   d. confederate   _____

2. **revise** the schedule
   a. discharge   b. pursue   c. modify   d. swindle   _____

3. **aim for** a career in medicine
   a. modify   b. discharge   c. swindle   d. pursue   _____

4. an ironclad **excuse**
   a. confederate   b. reign   c. alibi   d. mutiny   _____

5. a **regime** of terror
   a. swindle   b. discharge   c. mutiny   d. reign   _____

6. **cheated** by a con artist
   a. pursued   b. swindled   c. modified   d. discharged   _____

Antonyms

*For each item below, choose the word that is most nearly **opposite** in meaning to the word or phrase in **boldface**. Then write your choice on the line provided.*

1. **positive** numbers
   a. negative   b. singular   c. economical   d. confederate   _____

2. the **wasteful** use of natural resources
   a. frank   b. economical   c. singular   d. negative   _____

3. soldiers who **obey**
   a. discharge   b. mutiny   c. reign   d. swindle   _____

4. **load** a cannon
   a. modify   b. pursue   c. swindle   d. discharge   _____

5. **plural** nouns
   a. negative   b. economical   c. singular   d. frank   _____

6. **enemies** of the tribe
   a. reigns   b. alibis   c. mutinies   d. confederates   _____

Completing the Sentence

From the list of words on pages 122–123, choose the one that best completes each item below. Write the word in the space provided. (You may have to change the word's ending.)

■ When I write an essay, I start with a rough draft. Then I review what I have written to see how I can improve it. One way that I may _____ the essay is to get rid of any repetitions.

■ Because I want to keep the reader's attention, I try to keep my sentences clear and brief. Therefore, I look for more _____ ways to make my points.

■ For example, if I am writing about two people, I may want to use the plural pronoun *they* instead of _____ pronouns such as *he* and *she*. As a last step I reread the essay to make sure there are no errors of spelling, grammar, or punctuation.

TROUBLE ON THE HIGH SEAS

■ Captain William Bligh, an English admiral, _____ over his ship, the *Bounty,* as if he were its king.

■ His harsh treatment and mean-spirited rules aroused _____ feelings among crew members. Few viewed the captain in a favorable light.

■ In a secret but _____ discussion, the sailors plotted to take over the ship.

■ A ship's officer named Fletcher Christian seized control of the *Bounty* on April 28, 1789. This daring _____ has been the subject of several popular movies.

CRIME AT THE CASH MACHINE

■ Soon after my uncle opened a checking account at a new bank, he was the victim of a bank machine _____.

■ A woman posing as a banker and her _____, who said he was the manager, advised my uncle to get $200 from the cash machine to test his bank card. The crooks then ran off with my uncle's money.

■ Using the descriptions given by my uncle and a witness, the police _____ the two thieves on foot, catching up to them a few blocks away.

■ They soon arrested the suspects without having to _____ their weapons.

■ At their trial the two thieves claimed that they were innocent. But the jury did not believe their _____. It took the jury only fifteen minutes to find them guilty.

Word Associations

*Circle the letter next to the word or expression that best completes the sentence or answers the question. Pay special attention to the word in **boldface**.*

1. A **frank** comment is
   a. always complimentary
   b. never hurtful
   c. always appreciated
   d. never dishonest

2. An **economical** car probably
   a. stalls frequently
   b. uses little gas
   c. pollutes the air
   d. runs on air

3. Infantry soldiers who **mutiny** are likely to
   a. get medals
   b. be promoted
   c. get new uniforms
   d. be punished

4. To **modify** a drawing you might
   a. erase a few lines
   b. crumple it up
   c. show it to a friend
   d. go to a museum

5. Which of these is a good **alibi**?
   a. "I didn't do it."
   b. "I was in school at that time."
   c. "I saw them rob the store."
   d. "I hope you catch the crook."

6. Which of these is a **singular** noun?
   a. chicks
   b. geese
   c. goose
   d. ducks

7. A **negative** person is likely to
   a. take great vacation pictures
   b. be good at math
   c. find fault with any plan
   d. see the best in everyone

8. A **reigning** king probably has
   a. boots and an umbrella
   b. a scepter and a crown
   c. a computer and a modem
   d. a bow and an arrow

9. If I **swindle** my little brother, I
   a. cheat him
   b. read to him
   c. protect him
   d. draw a picture of him

10. A factory is likely to **discharge**
    a. prisoners
    b. metal parts
    c. rifles
    d. smoke

11. I would expect my **confederates** to
    a. work together with me
    b. make fun of me
    c. refuse to help me
    d. plot against me

12. Which of these is a cat most likely to **pursue**?
    a. a dream
    b. a mouse
    c. a dog
    d. a career in television

Definitions

Study the spelling, pronunciation, part of speech, and definition given for each of the words below. Write the word in the blank space in the sentence that follows. Then read the synonyms and antonyms.

1. **complicate**
   (käm′ plə kāt)

   (v.) to make hard to understand or do
   A lot of unnecessary details can sometimes _____ directions.

   SYNONYMS: to confuse, muddle, mix up
   ANTONYMS: to simplify, clarify, smooth, ease

2. **courteous**
   (kûr′ tē əs)

   (adj.) considerate toward others
   A _____ host is sure to greet all guests and make them feel welcome.

   SYNONYMS: polite, well-mannered, respectful, civil
   ANTONYMS: rude, impolite, ill-mannered, discourteous

3. **discomfort**
   (dis kum′ fərt)

   (n.) a lack of ease and well-being
   A nasty case of chicken pox can cause a great deal of _____.

   SYNONYMS: pain, distress, irritation, suffering
   ANTONYMS: comfort, peace, calm

4. **eliminate**
   (i li′ mə nāt)

   (v.) to get rid of or do away with
   If we all work together, we can _____ hunger and poverty.

   SYNONYMS: to remove, omit, leave out, exclude, drop
   ANTONYMS: to take in, admit, acquire, retain, preserve

5. **grieve**
   (grēv)

   (v.) to cause to feel great sadness; to feel very sad
   Reports of the many deaths and the destruction caused by the earthquake _____ us all.

   SYNONYMS: to sadden, mourn, regret
   ANTONYMS: to rejoice, celebrate, gladden

6. **moral**
   (môr′ əl)

   (adj.) having to do with what is right and wrong; being good and just
   A _____ question is sometimes very difficult to answer.
   (n.) the lesson taught by a story or experience
   I think that the _____ of the story is "never give up."

   SYNONYMS: (adj.) honorable, upright, honest; (n.) a message, teaching
   ANTONYMS: (adj.) immoral, wicked, bad, wrong

Millions of people visit New York every year to view the **spectacle** (word 9) of the Manhattan skyline.

7. scorch
(skôrch)

(v.) to burn on the surface; to dry out with heat

Did you _____ my brand-new shirt with the iron?

(n.) a slight burn

I placed the napkin so it would cover a _____ in the tablecloth.

SYNONYMS: (v.) to singe, brown, blacken, shrivel

8. severe
(sə vēr')

(adj.) of a serious nature; very strict and harsh; causing pain or hardship

Most parents think lying is a _____ offense.

SYNONYMS: grave, stern; tough, bitter; brutal, rough
ANTONYMS: unimportant; mild; merciful

9. spectacle
(spek' ti kəl)

(n.) an unusual sight or public display

An eclipse of the sun is an awesome _____.

SYNONYMS: a scene, show, exhibition, marvel

10. tragic
(tra' jik)

(adj.) having to do with a serious story with a sad ending; very unfortunate

Stories with _____ endings make me cry.

SYNONYMS: dreadful, awful, sad, disastrous, unhappy
ANTONYMS: amusing, funny, humorous, comical, happy

11. trifle
(trī' fəl)

(n.) something of little importance; a small amount

It is not worth arguing over such a _____.

(v.) to treat carelessly or playfully

It is unkind to _____ with someone's feelings.

SYNONYMS: (n.) a bit, knickknack, trinket; (v.) to fiddle, play, toy
ANTONYMS: (n.) a lot, lots of

12. universal
(yü nə vûr' səl)

(adj.) being everywhere; of, for, or shared by all

Food and shelter are _____ needs.

SYNONYMS: worldwide, broad, general, widespread
ANTONYMS: local, limited, narrow

Match the Meaning

For each item below, choose the word whose meaning is suggested by the clue given. Then write the word in the space provided.

1. To feel great sadness over a loss is to _____.
   a. scorch   b. trifle   c. grieve   d. eliminate

2. When you make a task harder, you _____ it.
   a. complicate   b. eliminate   c. scorch   d. grieve for

3. If your throat is sore, you might feel _____.
   a. moral   b. discomfort   c. scorch   d. spectacle

4. Joy that is shared by everyone in the world is _____.
   a. tragic   b. severe   c. universal   d. moral

5. Someone who is considerate of other people's feelings is _____.
   a. courteous   b. moral   c. severe   d. tragic

6. During a dry spell the sun may _____ the earth.
   a. complicate   b. eliminate   c. trifle with   d. scorch

7. A fatal accident is a _____ event.
   a. moral   b. courteous   c. tragic   d. universal

8. A very strict or harsh king is a _____ ruler.
   a. universal   b. severe   c. courteous   d. tragic

9. A life that is good and just is a _____ one.
   a. moral   b. severe   c. tragic   d. universal

10. A small amount of something is a _____.
   a. discomfort   b. moral   c. spectacle   d. trifle

11. To get rid of something is to _____ it.
   a. complicate   b. grieve for   c. trifle with   d. eliminate

12. A public display, such as fireworks, is a _____.
   a. trifle   b. spectacle   c. discomfort   d. moral

For each item below, choose the word that is most nearly the **same** in meaning as the word or phrase in **boldface.** Then write your choice on the line provided.

1. caused great **distress**
   a. spectacle   b. trifle   c. discomfort   d. moral   _____

2. a grand **scene**
   a. moral   b. spectacle   c. trifle   d. discomfort   _____

3. the **message** of the fable
   a. trifle   b. scorch   c. spectacle   d. moral   _____

4. **burned** the grass
   a. scorched   b. eliminated   c. complicated   d. grieved for   _____

5. **fiddle** with the rules
   a. complicate   b. scorch   c. eliminate   d. trifle   _____

6. **leave out** the negative comments
   a. eliminate   b. complicate   c. trifle with   d. grieve for   _____

For each item below, choose the word that is most nearly **opposite** in meaning to the word or phrase in **boldface.** Then write your choice on the line provided.

1. **simplify** things
   a. scorch   b. complicate   c. eliminate   d. trifle with   _____

2. a **mild** winter
   a. severe   b. moral   c. universal   d. courteous   _____

3. having **limited** appeal
   a. tragic   b. severe   c. moral   d. universal   _____

4. **amusing** love stories
   a. universal   b. courteous   c. tragic   d. moral   _____

5. a **rude** customer
   a. severe   b. universal   c. courteous   d. tragic   _____

6. **rejoice** with the family
   a. trifle   b. grieve   c. scorch   d. eliminate   _____

Completing the Sentence

From the list of words on pages 128–129, choose the one that best completes each item below. Then write the word in the space provided. (You may have to change the word's ending.)

DEATH OF A PRESIDENT

■ When President John F. Kennedy was killed by an assassin's bullet on November 22, 1963, the _____ event shocked the nation. The President was only forty-five years old.

■ Americans _____ openly as they watched his formal state funeral on television or listened to it on the radio.

■ People still recall the respectful and _____ behavior of the huge crowds that lined the funeral route.

WHY SAVE THE RAIN FORESTS?

■ The magnificent variety of animals and plants in the tropical rain forests creates a _____ unlike anything else in nature.

■ The effort to protect these forests is _____ by the need to use some of the valuable resources found in them, such as medicines.

■ When any plant or animal is forever _____ from the earth, the balance of nature changes. The loss of a single species may result in harm to many more.

■ One result of a change in the balance of nature can be a _____ shift in weather patterns. A change that at first has only local effects may in time affect the whole world.

■ Many people now regard destruction of the rain forests as a _____ issue, not just a political or legal one, because it can ruin the future of the entire planet.

SUNBURN REALLY HURTS

■ Many people do not realize how easily they can _____ their skin just by walking or playing outside on a sunny day.

■ Even on a cloudy day, it is possible to get a _____ sunburn.

■ If you get a painful sunburn, ask your doctor what you should do to ease the

_____ .

■ Always remember that a sunburn is nothing to _____ with. It can cause serious harm to your skin.

Word Associations

*Circle the letter next to the word or expression that best completes the sentence or answers the question. Pay special attention to the word in **boldface**.*

1. A **courteous** bus driver might
   a. yell at passengers
   b. greet each passenger
   c. wear gloves while driving
   d. pass your bus stop on purpose

2. A **severe** cold spell would
   a. cause great hardship
   b. delight all skiers
   c. make people sleepy
   d. not last long

3. A **tragic** event might make you
   a. jump for joy
   b. break a leg
   c. weep with sadness
   d. go to a movie

4. If you feel **discomfort,** you should
   a. turn off the lights
   b. whistle in the dark
   c. rest for an hour
   d. seek relief

5. Which of these is a **universal** human experience?
   a. raising camels
   b. becoming an astronaut
   c. owning a rice plantation
   d. being born

6. Which is the **moral** of a story?
   a. "Slow and steady wins the race."
   b. "Do not fold, tear, or cut."
   c. "Dogs are related to wolves."
   d. "Why can't people fly?"

7. A **complicated** explanation is
   a. easy to understand
   b. likely to be false
   c. always helpful
   d. hard to follow

8. **Scorched** milk is sure to taste
   a. spicy
   b. sweet
   c. burnt
   d. refreshing

9. To **eliminate** sugar from your diet, you can
   a. add more salt
   b. learn how to cook
   c. cut out sweets
   d. drink lots of water

10. Which of these is a **trifle**?
    a. a party favor
    b. a huge weapon
    c. a million dollars
    d. a banquet

11. Which is a **spectacle**?
    a. a pair of glasses
    b. a three-ring circus
    c. an empty football field
    d. a bowl of vanilla ice cream

12. People usually **grieve** at
    a. birthday parties
    b. family funerals
    c. political rallies
    d. baseball games

Definitions

Study the spelling, pronunciation, part of speech, and definition given for each of the words below. Write the word in the blank space in the sentence that follows. Then read the synonyms and antonyms.

1. **assume**
   (ə süm')

   (v.) to take upon oneself; to take for oneself; to pretend to have or be; to take for granted
   > *My parents said I could have the puppy if I would _____ the responsibility for it.*

   SYNONYMS: to accept, undertake, seize; to imagine, suppose, believe
   ANTONYMS: to reject, refuse, give up

2. **cram**
   (kram)

   (v.) to stuff tightly; to fill tightly; to study hard just before a test
   > *Mom told me not to _____ all my clothes into one drawer.*

   SYNONYMS: to pack, crowd, jam, load, squeeze
   ANTONYMS: to empty, clean out, clear out

3. **endanger**
   (in dān' jər)

   (v.) to expose to injury or harm
   > *Fire and drought _____ our forests and the animals that live in them.*

   SYNONYMS: to risk, threaten
   ANTONYMS: to protect, defend, preserve, save, secure

4. **fare**
   (fâr)

   (v.) to get along
   > *If you study hard, you should _____ well in school.*

   (n.) the cost of travel on public transportation; food and drink
   > *Dad called to find out the plane _____ from Los Angeles to New York.*

   SYNONYMS: (v.) to manage, succeed; (n.) a charge, fee, price; a menu

5. **fertile**
   (fûr' təl)

   (adj.) good for producing crops and plants; capable of developing or growing
   > *The rich farmland of the Midwest makes it one of the most _____ areas in the world.*

   SYNONYMS: fruitful, productive, rich
   ANTONYMS: barren, unproductive

6. **furnish**
   (fûr' nish)

   (v.) to supply with furniture; to supply with what is needed
   > *After the fire damage was repaired, neighbors pitched in to help _____ the house.*

   SYNONYMS: to equip, outfit, provide, give
   ANTONYMS: to take, withhold

One of the most **fertile** (word 5) areas in the world is the Midwest, sometimes called "America's Breadbasket."

7. **mammoth**
(ma′ məth)

(n.) a very large, long-tusked, shaggy-haired elephant that is now extinct
The last woolly _____ *died thousands of years ago.*
(adj.) great in size
A skyscraper is a _____ *building.*
SYNONYMS: (adj.) enormous, huge, immense, gigantic, colossal
ANTONYMS: (adj.) small, tiny, little, miniature

8. **peer**
(pēr)

(n.) a person of the same age, rank, or ability; a British noble
As a gifted pianist, the child had no _____.
(v.) to look closely at
I tend to _____ *at people through my glasses.*
SYNONYMS: (n.) an equal, colleague; (v.) to gaze, stare, scan

9. **rigid**
(ri′ jəd)

(adj.) not bending; very strict
Stand at attention, and keep your body _____.
SYNONYMS: stiff, firm, inflexible; severe, stern
ANTONYMS: elastic, flexible, loose

10. **rowdy**
(raủ′ dē)

(adj.) rough and disorderly
My teacher does not tolerate _____ *behavior.*
SYNONYMS: wild, unruly, noisy
ANTONYMS: quiet, tame, gentle, mild

11. **safeguard**
(sāf′ gärd)

(n.) something that protects
A helmet is a _____ *against head injuries.*
(v.) to protect against possible danger
Wear sunblock to _____ *your skin.*
SYNONYMS: (n.) a protection, defense; (v.) to defend, guard, save
ANTONYMS: (v.) to endanger, threaten, risk

12. **trespass**
(n., tres′ pəs;
v., tres′ pas)

(n.) an action that is wrong; unlawful entry onto someone's property
The man was charged with criminal _____.
(v.) to do wrong; to enter onto someone's property without right
I did not mean to _____ *against you.*
SYNONYMS: (n.) a sin, wrongdoing; an invasion; (v.) to sin, offend, intrude

135

For each item below, choose the word whose meaning is suggested by the clue given. Then write the word in the space provided.

1. If I put people at risk, I _____ their lives.
   a. cram   b. safeguard   c. assume   d. endanger

2. A noisy and wild party may be described as _____.
   a. mammoth   b. rowdy   c. fertile   d. rigid

3. A member of British royalty is a _____.
   a. peer   b. safeguard   c. mammoth   d. fare

4. To take something for granted is to _____ it is so.
   a. cram   b. assume   c. furnish   d. endanger

5. When I eat bread and cheese for lunch, I dine on simple _____.
   a. safeguards   b. mammoths   c. fare   d. trespasses

6. A large, extinct "woolly" elephant is called a _____.
   a. mammoth   b. safeguard   c. peer   d. fare

7. If a lot of people get on a bus or train, they _____ into it.
   a. furnish   b. assume   c. safeguard   d. cram

8. A person who is very strict may be described as _____.
   a. rowdy   b. rigid   c. mammoth   d. fertile

9. If I protect people from risk, I _____ their lives.
   a. assume   b. endanger   c. safeguard   d. furnish

10. An egg that can develop into a chick is one that is _____.
    a. fertile   b. rowdy   c. mammoth   d. rigid

11. To enter someone's property without first getting permission is to _____.
    a. cram   b. endanger   c. trespass   d. peer

12. If I supply necessary information, I _____ the facts.
    a. safeguard   b. endanger   c. assume   d. furnish

Synonyms

*For each item below, choose the word that is most nearly the **same** in meaning as the word or phrase in **boldface**. Then write your choice on the line provided.*

1. **stare** through the window

   a. cram   b. trespass   c. peer   d. assume   _____

2. **rich** soil

   a. rigid   b. fertile   c. rowdy   d. mammoth   _____

3. **defend** the planet

   a. furnish   b. endanger   c. cram   d. safeguard   _____

4. collect the **fee**

   a. mammoth   b. fare   c. safeguard   d. peer   _____

5. **equip** the lab

   a. furnish   b. endanger   c. cram   d. safeguard   _____

6. **intrude** on private property

   a. peer   b. assume   c. trespass   d. cram   _____

Antonyms

*For each item below, choose the word that is most nearly **opposite** in meaning to the word or phrase in **boldface**. Then write your choice on the line provided.*

1. **small** in size

   a. rigid   b. mammoth   c. rowdy   d. fertile   _____

2. a **quiet** activity

   a. rigid   b. fertile   c. mammoth   d. rowdy   _____

3. a **flexible** rule

   a. mammoth   b. rowdy   c. fertile   d. rigid   _____

4. **empty** your locker

   a. furnish   b. safeguard   c. cram   d. endanger   _____

5. **protect** the spotted owl

   a. cram   b. endanger   c. furnish   d. safeguard   _____

6. **give up** control

   a. furnish   b. safeguard   c. assume   d. endanger   _____

Completing the Sentence

From the list of words on pages 134–135, choose the one that best completes each item below. Write the word in the space provided. (You may have to change the word's ending.)

From the list of words on pages 134–135

A BIG MISTAKE

■ I made a big mistake when I _____ that I could wait until the night before the big test to start studying. I should have known better than to take it for granted that I would do well on the test.

■ My _____ teased me when I told them that I was worried about the test. They said I didn't need to study hard. Now I know that I shouldn't have listened to them.

■ I had to stay up very late to _____ my brain full of facts and figures. When I realized how much I needed to learn, I began to feel sick with panic.

■ To make matters worse, the people in the house next door had a _____ party that lasted until one o'clock in the morning. I couldn't sleep because of the noise.

■ The next day I was so tired that I couldn't remember anything. So it was no surprise that I _____ badly on the test.

SAVE THE WETLANDS

■ America's wetlands provide a rich and _____ environment for thousands of species of plants and animals.

■ But pollution and development more and more _____ these beautiful places. In some areas their very survival is at risk.

■ If we lose our wetlands, many of the creatures that live there will become as extinct as the woolly _____.

■ Lots of concerned individuals and organizations are working to educate the public about how important it is to _____ this precious natural resource.

SAFETY IN A DANGEROUS PLACE

■ Scientists who study deadly viruses work in special laboratories where strict safety measures are enforced. There are _____ rules to protect all the employees.

■ All workers are _____ with special protective clothing that they must put on before going into the lab.

■ Only employees are allowed to enter the lab. Anyone who tries to get into one of these "hot zones" without proper identification will be considered to be _____. Security guards will escort intruders from the building.

Word Associations

*Circle the letter next to the word or expression that best completes the sentence or answers the question. Pay special attention to the word in **boldface**.*

1. A **fertile** animal may give birth to
   a. many young
   b. green plants
   c. good ideas
   d. fruits or vegetables

2. A jury of your **peers** would be made up of
   a. two dukes
   b. your parents
   c. other students
   d. telescopes

3. A **rowdy** greeting is likely to be
   a. stern
   b. loud
   c. gentle
   d. whispered

4. Which is a **safeguard** against theft?
   a. a burglar alarm
   b. sunscreen
   c. lifeguard
   d. deodorant soap

5. Which usually requires paying a **fare**?
   a. a skateboard ride
   b. a taxi ride
   c. a car ride
   d. a sled ride

6. One who **assumes** a brave manner is
   a. bragging
   b. fighting
   c. shouting
   d. pretending

7. A **crammed** suitcase is probably
   a. well organized
   b. half full
   c. hard to close
   d. locked

8. One way to say "No **Trespassing**" is
   a. "Closed for Repairs"
   b. "Keep Out"
   c. "Out of Business"
   d. "This Way to Exit"

9. If I **furnish** food for a picnic, I
   a. invite the ants
   b. set up the lawn furniture
   c. eat the lion's share
   d. bring lots to eat

10. A **mammoth** corporation probably has
    a. a large board of directors
    b. many elephants
    c. lions, tigers, and bears
    d. a small parking lot

11. An **endangered** species is
    a. threatened by extinction
    b. dangerous to others
    c. safe from harm
    d. protected by mammoths

12. Which of these is **rigid**?
    a. a rubber band
    b. a mound of jello
    c. a soap bubble
    d. a steel beam

Selecting Word Meanings

For each of the following items, circle the choice that is most nearly the **same** in meaning as the word in **boldface** type in the introductory phrase.

1. an important scientific **achievement**
   a. failure   b. principle   c. method   d. accomplishment

2. **furnish** proof of ownership
   a. supply   b. copy   c. lose   d. request

3. an inexpensive **trifle**
   a. gift   b. trinket   c. meal   d. weapon

4. a **singular** opportunity
   a. welcome   b. missed   c. unusual   d. lucky

5. a **moral** decision
   a. wicked   b. reasonable   c. just   d. difficult

6. arrested the **confederates**
   a. accomplices   b. witnesses   c. victims   d. enemies

7. **swindle** the tourist
   a. help   b. cheat   c. meet   d. entertain

8. **grieved** for the victims
   a. worked   b. rejoiced   c. searched   d. mourned

9. **endanger** the public's health
   a. ignore   b. protect   c. threaten   d. study

10. **sanitary** medical instruments
    a. filthy   b. sterile   c. new   d. used

11. an **economical** means of transportation
    a. thrifty   b. safe   c. comfortable   d. costly

12. a bitter **debate**
    a. medicine   b. person   c. taste   d. argument

Spelling

For each item below, study the **boldface** word in which there is a blank. If a letter is missing, fill in the blank to make a correctly spelled word. If the word is already spelled correctly, leave the blank empty.

1. **spra__l** in a hammock

2. **tres__pass** on my land

3. **re__gn** over France

4. a **ro__wdy** mob

5. a **tra__ic** mistake

6. **a__quire** knowledge

7. a **fertil__** imagination

8. **s__orch** the linen

9. **safeg__ard** the passengers

10. a **mono__tonous** story

11. **mod__fy** the instructions

12. **elim__nate** the problem

Antonyms

For each of the following items, circle the choice that is most nearly the **opposite** in meaning to the word in **boldface** type in the introductory phrase.

1. the **latter** part of the year
   a. earlier
   b. warmest
   c. last
   d. largest

2. show signs of **discomfort**
   a. excitement
   b. irritation
   c. interest
   d. calm

3. **cram** the theater aisles
   a. crowd
   b. clear out
   c. stand in
   d. walk down

4. a **courteous** note
   a. unsigned
   b. polite
   c. short
   d. rude

5. **preserve** the landmark building
   a. save
   b. paint
   c. destroy
   d. enlarge

6. rise up in **mutiny**
   a. support
   b. song
   c. rebellion
   d. anger

7. **complicate** the assignment
   a. confuse
   b. complete
   c. change
   d. simplify

8. a **negative** attitude
   a. friendly
   b. positive
   c. bad
   d. peculiar

Vocabulary for Comprehension

Read the following passage in which some of the words you have studied appear in **boldface**. *Then answer the questions on page 143.*

The Experience of a Lifetime

Carl, Anna, and their parents joined the crowd in the station. They had prepared for this day since March. Carl earned money doing the morning milking. Anna baked pies and biscuits. The family was careful to save every penny toward the train **fare** and the admission fee. At last, they were ready for the greatest celebration of the century—the 1893 Chicago World's Fair. They joined travelers from all over the world, eager to see the **spectacle** on Lake Michigan.

The train was nearly full when it entered the station. The crowd was quick to board. Anna clutched Carl's hand as Mom and Dad guided them toward a seat. After an hour's rattling ride, the train was at the fair's main gate.

Carl whistled. Anna gasped in awe. Tens of thousands of visitors were strolling the walkways. People toured halls **crammed** with **exhibits**. Anna and Carl stopped to see a gigantic cheese from Canada. It weighed in at 22,000 pounds! "C'mon, kids," Dad exclaimed. "Let's find the trained lions from Africa, the electric dishwashing machine, and the United States map that's made entirely of pickles!"

"First, the wheel," said Carl with enthusiasm.

"The wheel?" Anna asked.

Ferris wheel on the grounds of the 1893 World's Fair

"You know. The one by George Ferris, the genius engineer from Pittsburgh," Carl answered. "Maybe we can ride twice!"

The family headed toward the wondrous wheel, which towered over everything else. It was huge! Its 36 wooden cars carried 2,160 people high above the ground for a thrilling 20-minute view of the **sprawling** exhibition grounds. Carl and Anna took their places on the long line for the ride of a lifetime.

Fill in the circle next to the choice that best completes the sentence or answers the question.

1. This passage was mainly written to
   - ⓐ encourage tourism to Chicago
   - ⓑ provide a glimpse into the future
   - ⓒ describe the creation of the Ferris wheel
   - ⓓ provide a picture of the World's Fair of 1893

2. The events take place at
   - ⓐ the fairgrounds in Chicago
   - ⓑ a lake in Canada
   - ⓒ an amusement park in Michigan
   - ⓓ a train station in Pittsburgh

3. In this passage, **fare** means
   - ⓐ manage
   - ⓑ charge
   - ⓒ menu
   - ⓓ route

4. A **spectacle** is a(n)
   - ⓐ luxury boat
   - ⓑ grand public display
   - ⓒ dance performance
   - ⓓ impressive sunrise

5. From the passage, you can tell that Carl and Anna live
   - ⓐ on or near a farm
   - ⓑ in an apartment house
   - ⓒ in Chicago
   - ⓓ near Lake Michigan

6. When Carl and Anna were roaming the fair, you could say they were
   - ⓐ displeased
   - ⓑ overjoyed
   - ⓒ fearful
   - ⓓ frantic

7. Another word for **crammed** is
   - ⓐ packed
   - ⓑ furnished
   - ⓒ littered
   - ⓓ preserved

8. The **exhibits** in this passage are
   - ⓐ paintings from an art class
   - ⓑ displays shown to the public
   - ⓒ preserves for wild animals
   - ⓓ amazing stories

9. According to Carl, the highlight of the fair is the
   - ⓐ trained lions
   - ⓑ gigantic cheese
   - ⓒ electric dishwashing machine
   - ⓓ Ferris wheel

10. **Sprawling** most nearly means
   - ⓐ narrow
   - ⓑ scenic
   - ⓒ spread out
   - ⓓ elaborate

Grammar in Context

A **verb** and its **subject** must **agree** in number. This means that if the subject is singular, the verb must be singular. If the subject is plural, the verb must be plural.

The verb **be** does not show action. It tells what the subject is or is like. Use the form of **be** that agrees with the subject.

Subject	Present Tense	Past Tense
I	am	was
he, she, it, or singular noun	is	was
you, we, they, or plural noun	are	were

Read the sentences in the box. Notice how the subject and verb in each sentence agree.

> The crowd was quick to board.   We are thrilled.
>
> People were ready for the celebration.   He is a genius.

*Choose the verb in **boldface** that correctly completes the sentence. Then write the sentence on the line.*

1. Anna (**is, are**) grateful for the invitation to the exhibit. _____

_____

2. Carl (**was, were**) courteous and thanked the man. _____

_____

3. The mammoth displays (**was, were**) magnificent. _____

_____

4. The metal frames (**is, are**) a little rusty but still rigid. _____

_____

5. The fair (**was, were**) an enormous achievement. _____

_____

Completing the Idea

*Complete each sentence so that it makes sense. Pay attention to the word in **boldface**.*

1. The crowd became **rowdy** when _____.

2. When I **acquire** my new bike, I will _____.

3. It is so **monotonous** to listen to _____.

4. One way to maintain **sanitary** conditions is to _____.

5. To be perfectly **frank**, I wish _____.

6. I want to **modify** my speech because _____.

7. I might **pursue** a job in which I _____.

8. Three examples of **singular** nouns are _____.

9. To do well on the test, I must **furnish** _____.

10. New shoes may cause great **discomfort** because _____.

11. You might **scorch** the toast if you _____.

12. It is normal to **grieve** after _____.

13. In **fertile** soil, you can expect to _____.

14. Use a small mirror to **peer** into _____.

15. When a sign says "Do Not **Trespass**," you'd better _____.

Write Your Own
*Choose a word from Units 13–16. Write a sentence using the word.
Be sure to correct any errors in subject-verb agreement.*

_____

_____

Word Families

*The words in **boldface** in the sentences below are related to words introduced in Units 13–16. For example, the adjectives trifling and spectacular in item 1 are related to the nouns trifle and spectacle (both in Unit 15). Based on your understanding of the unit words that follow, circle the related word in **boldface** that best completes each sentence.*

acquire	assume	complicate	courteous	eliminate
exhibit	furnish	modify	monotonous	moral
preserve	pursue	rigid	rowdy	severe
singular	spectacle	tragic	trifle	universal

1. One reason for a movie's success at the box office may be its (**trifling/ spectacular**) special effects.

2. Several rooms in the museum display (**furnishings/complications**) from colonial America.

3. Scientists all over the world are working for the (**preservation/assumption**) of endangered animals such as the giant panda, the tiger, and the tamarins of the Amazon rain forests.

4. Americans believe that the (**courtesy/pursuit**) of happiness is a basic human right.

5. Because of the (**severity/rowdiness**) of the blizzard, highways were closed, and flights were canceled.

6. Museum officials held a press conference to announce the (**modification/ acquisition**) of an important painting by Picasso.

7. Last fall my English class attended a performance of a (**tragedy/morality**) by William Shakespeare.

8. When I have a boring chore to do, I like to listen to music to relieve the (**monotony/singularity**) of the task.

9. A highlight of this year's science fair was an (**elimination/exhibition**) of crystals and minerals.

10. The popular author's new novel was widely praised for the (**universality/ rigidity**) of its story.

Word Games

Use the clue and the given letters to complete each word. Write the missing letters of the word in the appropriate boxes. Then use the circled letters and the drawing to find the CHALLENGE word.

1. Rather unusual!

(⃝) (☐) N G ☐ ☐ ☐ (⃝)

2. An occasion for pro and con

☐ (⃝) ☐ (⃝) T ☐

3. Another word for an English noble

(⃝) E ☐ ☐

4. How would you describe a person who is polite and thoughtful?

☐ ☐ U ☐ T ☐ ☐ ☐ (⃝)

5. Don't bother me with such an unimportant matter.

(⃝) ☐ ☐ F ☐ ☐

6. A hospital operating room should always be this.

(⃝) ☐ N ☐ ☐ ☐ ☐ Y

Challenge:

If I disobey this sign, what would I do?

☐ ☐ ☐ ☐ ☐ ☐ ☐ ☐

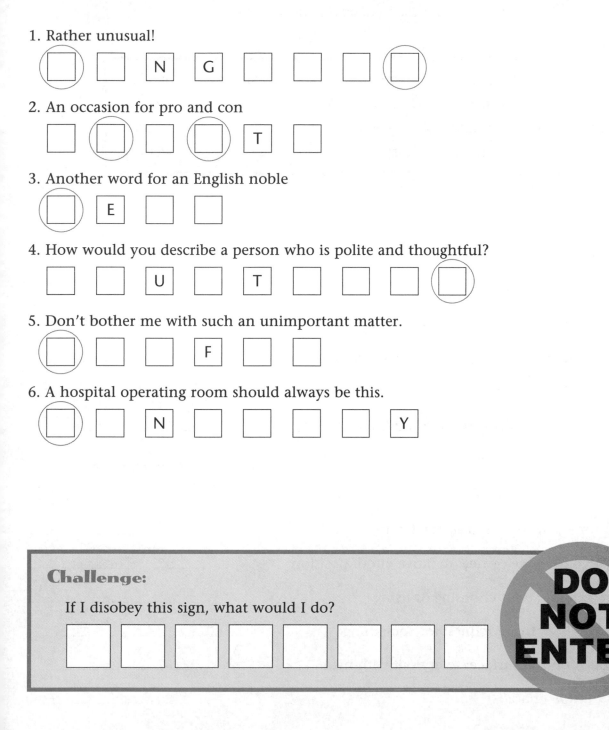

Definitions *Choose the word from the box that matches each definition. Write the word on the line provided.*

abolish	abuse	appeal	avalanche	brittle
dictator	displace	gauge	massacre	migrant
nestle	portable	preserve	rigid	scorch
selective	singular	spectacle	tragic	vicinity

1. an unusual sight or public display _____

2. to settle down comfortably; to hold lovingly _____

3. not bending; very strict _____

4. a ruler or leader who has total power _____

5. to kill many people or animals in a cruel way _____

6. out of the ordinary _____

7. the area near a place, the surrounding region _____

8. to measure; to estimate _____

9. easily moved or carried _____

10. improper, wrong, or cruel treatment _____

11. to force to move or flee; to move out of position _____

12. very careful about choosing or using _____

13. a sincere or strong request for something _____

14. to burn on the surface; to dry out with heat _____

15. very unfortunate _____

 **Antonyms**

*Choose the word from the box that is most nearly **opposite** in meaning to each group of words. Write the word on the line provided.*

1. divided, separated; a foe   _____

2. unlike, different   _____

3. to lose, give up, surrender   _____

4. quiet, tame, gentle   _____

5. feast, plenty   _____

6. kindhearted, merciful   _____

7. to hate, despise, dishonor   _____

8. local, limited, narrow   _____

9. to detain; to hire; to load   _____

10. a defeat, failure, setback   _____

11. barren, unproductive   _____

12. to run away (from), flee   _____

13. sensible, wise, intelligent   _____

14. a hunter, predator   _____

15. wicked, bad, wrong   _____

16. to protect, defend, preserve   _____

17. varied, lively, exciting   _____

18. to rejoice, celebrate, gladden   _____

19. slow, dull, sluggish   _____

20. to shrink, reduce, contract   _____

absurd
achievement
acquire
brisk
cherish
confederate
discharge
downfall
endanger
expand
famine
fertile
grieve
humiliate
identical
monotonous
moral
negative
pitiless
prey
pursue
rowdy
safeguard
security
universal

Completing the Sentence

Choose the word from the box that best completes each sentence below. Write the word in the space provided.

Group A

courteous	descend	economical	flimsy
latter	modify	navigate	rotate

1. Believe it or not, it may be harder to _____ a steep hill than to climb it.

2. I carefully read the first part of the book, but I only skimmed the _____ half.

3. You're not a true sailor until you are able to _____ choppy waters.

4. You're likely to feel cold if you wear a(n) _____ jacket on a cool autumn night.

5. I waved to thank the _____ driver who let us cross the street.

Group B

alibi	confirm	fare	plea
principle	shred	soothe	trespass

1. I begged my parents to extend my curfew, but my _____ fell on deaf ears.

2. My teacher will not accept "The dog ate my homework" as a(n) _____ for not handing in an assignment.

3. I'll call the airline to _____ our reservations so we'll be sure to have seats on the flight.

4. You'll need exact change to pay the _____ when you board the bus.

5. Would you prefer creamy vanilla ice cream or hot tea with honey to _____ your sore throat?

Classifying

Choose the word from the box that goes best with each group of words. Write the word in the space provided. Then explain what the words have in common.

assume	daze	discomfort	foe	frank
mammoth	presentable	realistic	reign	tart

1. acceptable, enjoyable, _____

_____

2. dodo, passenger pigeon, saber-toothed tiger, _____

_____

3. bewilder, baffle, _____

_____

4. real, _____, reality, realize

_____

5. disorder, dishonor, _____

_____

6. blank, _____, sank, thank

_____

7. enemy, opponent, rival, _____

_____

8. rain, rein, _____

_____

9. cookie, muffin, cake, _____

_____

10. imagine, suppose, _____

_____

Analogies *In each of the following, circle the letter for the item that best completes the comparison. Then explain the relationship on the lines provided.*

1. **cherish** is to **abuse** as
   a. cuddle is to nestle
   b. displace is to move
   c. soothe is to excite
   d. end is to abolish

Relationship: _____

_____

_____

_____

2. **flimsy** is to **weak** as
   a. realistic is to absurd
   b. tart is to sweet
   c. selective is to choosy
   d. pitiless is to caring

Relationship: _____

_____

_____

_____

3. **attract** is to **appeal** as
   a. descend is to rise
   b. expand is to collapse
   c. plea is to forgive
   d. gauge is to measure

Relationship: _____

_____

_____

_____

4. **brittle** is to **flexible** as
   a. thrifty is to wasteful
   b. realistic is to practical
   c. tart is to tangy
   d. pitiless is to cruel

Relationship: _____

_____

_____

_____

5. **prey** is to **predator** as
   a. security is to doubt
   b. dictator is to tyrant
   c. plea is to appeal
   d. avalanche is to snow

Relationship: _____

_____

_____

_____

6. **famine** is to **food** as
   a. blizzard is to snow
   b. hurricane is to wind
   c. flood is to rain
   d. drought is to water

Relationship: _____

_____

_____

_____

7. **foe** is to **friend** as
   a. ally is to buddy
   b. moral is to message
   c. night is to day
   d. rest is to relaxation

Relationship: _____

_____

_____

_____

9. **present** is to **exhibit** as
   a. debate is to discuss
   b. reject is to accept
   c. stay is to leave
   d. fail is to succeed

Relationship: _____

_____

_____

_____

8. **humorous** is to **tragic** as
   a. speedy is to quick
   b. prepared is to ready
   c. clean is to sanitary
   d. mammoth is to miniature

Relationship: _____

_____

_____

_____

10. **mouse** is to **singular** as
   a. trap is to mouse
   b. mice is to plural
   c. mouse is to hole
   d. mice is to nice

Relationship: _____

_____

_____

_____

Challenge: Make up your own

Write a comparison using the words in the box below. (Hint: There are four possible analogies.) Then explain the relationship on the lines provided.

eat	fork	massacre	mutiny
negative	no	pencil	positive
revolt	slaughter	write	yes

Analogy: _____ is to _____ as _____ is to _____.

Relationship: _____

_____

_____

Building with Latin and Greek Roots

A **root** is the part of the word that carries its meaning. Sometimes knowing the meaning of a root can help you figure out the meaning of an unknown word.

> **spec**—look
>
> The root **spec** appears in **spectacle**. A **spectacle** is a sight that looks impressive or unusual.

*The words below contain the root **spec**. Study the definition of each word. Then write the word on the line in the sample sentence.*

1. **prospect**   something that is looked forward to or expected

    I'm excited by the _____ of getting a new bike.

2. **respect**   a high regard or consideration of the value of someone or something; to look at someone or something with high regard

    I _____ your opinion even though I don't agree with it.

3. **spectacular**   very unusual or impressive, making a great display

    The raging battle scenes in the film were _____.

4. **spectator**   a person who watches or looks but does not take part

    Not a single _____ left the final game of the World Series before the ninth inning.

5. **suspect**   to consider that something is true, likely, or possible; a person who is thought to be guilty of a crime

    I _____ that the store has already closed.

*Circle the word in **boldface** that best completes each sentence.*

1. We (**respect, suspect**) a trick is being played on us.

2. She earned everyone's (**prospect, respect**) for speaking out against the powerful politician.

3. The view of the Grand Canyon from the plane was (**spectacular, spectator**).

4. The (**prospect, suspect**) of moving to another country is both exciting and frightening.

5. Every (**spectacular, spectator**) gave the team a standing ovation.

From the list of words on page 154, choose the one that best completes each sentence below. Write the word on the line provided.

1. His fingerprints at the crime scene make him a prime ——————————— for the burglary.

2. The bursts of color in the fireworks display were ———————————!

3. I have great ——————————— for your honesty and openness.

4. A ——————————— from the visiting team waved her school banner at the game.

5. My sister is nervous about the ——————————— of attending a new school.

Definitions   *For each item, choose the word that matches the definition.*
Then write the word on the line provided.

1. to trick or lead a person into believing something that is not true

   a. blunder   b. displace   c. deceive   d. modify   _____

2. weariness or exhaustion from work or lack of sleep

   a. feat   b. assault   c. discomfort   d. fatigue   _____

3. not correct; showing bad manners or taste

   a. improper   b. aggressive   c. severe   d. rigid   _____

4. to stun or confuse

   a. dispute   b. daze   c. gauge   d. debate   _____

5. easily broken or damaged, requiring special handling or care

   a. keen   b. flimsy   c. rigid   d. fragile   _____

6. careful about spending money or using resources

   a. economical   b. moral   c. severe   d. energetic   _____

7. to cause to feel great sadness; to feel very sad

   a. enforce   b. justify   c. grieve   d. abuse   _____

8. lasting or used for a limited time

   a. temporary   b. presentable   c. economical   d. moral   _____

9. to stuff tightly; to fill tightly; to study hard just before a test

   a. distribute   b. bluff   c. classify   d. cram   _____

10. a discussion of reasons for and against something

    a. document   b. debate   c. plea   d. spectacle   _____

11. to plan or steer the course of a vessel or vehicle

    a. classify   b. emigrate   c. detect   d. navigate   _____

12. a partner, friend

    a. confederate   b. associate   c. nomad   d. monarch   _____

13. easily broken, snapped, or cracked; not flexible

    a. tart   b. rigid   c. vivid   d. brittle   _____

14. to turn around a central point; to alternate

    a. flexible   b. rotate   c. alternate   d. navigate   _____

15. to show clearly; to put on display

    a. exhibit   b. detect   c. alternate   d. discharge   _____

16. avoiding unnecessary risks or mistakes

    a. frank   b. moral   c. rowdy   d. cautious   _____

17. a friendly welcome and treatment of guests

    a. feat   b. hospitality   c. alibi   d. fare   _____

18. to force obedience to

    a. acquire   b. dispute   c. ensure   d. enforce   _____

19. to make calm; to ease pain or sorrow

    a. soothe   b. cherish   c. blunder   d. gauge   _____

20. rough and disorderly

    a. energetic   b. shrewd   c. capable   d. rowdy   _____

Antonyms   *For each item below, indicate the part of speech of the word in* **boldface**. *In the space provided, write* N *for noun,* V *for verb, or* A *for adjective.*

21. ____ felt the **jolt**

22. ____ a **supreme** effort

23. ____ **shred** the evidence

24. ____ joined the **mutiny**

25. ____ **cancel** the reservations

26. ____ fled the **famine**

27. ____ settle the **dispute**

28. ____ a **courteous** manner

29. ____ **sprawl** on the couch

30. ____ a **hearty** laugh

Completing the Sentence

Choose the word from the box that best completes each sentence. Write the word in the space provided. (You may have to change the word's ending.)

Group A

assume	cherish	confirm	fertile
postpone	reign	rigid	swindle

31. The mighty forces of nature can turn _____ farmland into a wasteland in which nothing will grow.

32. I will always _____ the memories of my visits to the Adirondacks.

33. It is the duty of the Senate to _____ or reject the President's appointments to the Supreme Court.

34. A team that _____ over a sport for several years is sometimes described as a "dynasty."

Group B

blemish	despise	feat	preserve
reliable	scorch	strategy	vast

35. The President promises to "_____, protect, and defend the Constitution of the United States."

36. Although the fire had _____ the letter, the writing could still be read.

37. It took many months for pioneers to cross the _____ stretches of the American plains.

38. The best _____ for taking a test is to study hard so that you are as prepared for it as you can be.

*Circle the letter next to the word or expression that best completes the sentence or answers the question. Pay special attention to the word in **boldface**.*

39. A **spectacle** might make you
    a. sleep
    b. fall
    c. stare
    d. eat

40. On a **bluff** you might
    a. go for a swim
    b. enjoy the view
    c. do your homework
    d. call a friend

41. Which should we **condemn**?
    a. cruelty
    b. kindness
    c. breakfast
    d. humor

42. Your **foe** is *not*
    a. your enemy
    b. your opponent
    c. your challenger
    d. your friend

43. Where would a **monarch** sit?
    a. on a throne
    b. in a court
    c. in a classroom
    d. in a highchair

44. Texas is in the **vicinity** of
    a. Canada
    b. India
    c. Mexico
    d. Spain

45. To **peer**, you need
    a. eyes
    b. ears
    c. thumbs
    d. toes

46. Who needs an **alibi**?
    a. a plumber
    b. a doctor
    c. a farmer
    d. a burglar

47. Which might you **classify**?
    a. trading cards
    b. pizzas
    c. sunsets
    d. gifts

48. With an **avalanche** comes
    a. good news
    b. mail
    c. snow
    d. coupons

49. A **solitary** walk is one
    a. that you take at night
    b. that you take barefoot
    c. that you take alone
    d. that you take after dinner

50. Which runs in a **primary**?
    a. a chicken
    b. a candidate
    c. a horse
    d. a dog

INDEX

The following is a list of all the words taught in the units of this book. The number after each entry indicates the page on which the word is first introduced, but the word also appears in exercises on later pages.

abandon, 18
abolish, 90
absurd, 96
abuse, 102
accomplish, 50
achievement, 116
acquire, 116
aggressive, 30
alibi, 122
alternate, 62
apparent, 50
appeal, 90
appliance, 102
assault, 18
associate, 30
assume, 134
avalanche, 96

barrier, 56
blemish, 44
bluff, 24
blunder, 12
blunt, 44
brisk, 84
brittle, 90

calculate, 56
cancel, 12
capable, 44
capacity, 50
cautious, 24
cherish, 84
civilian, 50
classify, 96
complicate, 128
compose, 56
conceal, 50
conclude, 44
condemn, 90
confederate, 122
confirm, 102
considerable, 56
considerate, 84

consist, 24
continuous, 12
convert, 18
courteous, 128
cram, 134

daze, 102
debate, 116
deceive, 30
demolish, 62
deputy, 56
descend, 90
despise, 24
detect, 44
dictator, 90
discharge, 122
discomfort, 128
displace, 84
dispute, 18
distribute, 12
document, 12
downfall, 84
duplicate, 50

economical, 122
eliminate, 128
emigrate, 30
endanger, 134
energetic, 62
enforce, 62
ensure, 96
estimate, 84
exhibit, 116
expand, 91

famine, 91
fare, 134
fatigue, 44
feat, 62
fertile, 134
festive, 45
flexible, 30
flimsy, 102

foe, 116
fragile, 12
frank, 122
furnish, 134

gauge, 102
glamour, 30
grieve, 128

haven, 24
hazy, 31
hearty, 62
hospitality, 45
humiliate, 85

identical, 85
impressive, 18
improper, 85
industrious, 56

jolt, 57
justify, 18

keen, 51

latter, 116
linger, 31
loot, 57
luxurious, 31

mammoth, 135
massacre, 117
mature, 63
migrant, 103
miniature, 24
mishap, 31
misleading, 19
modify, 122
monarch, 25
monotonous, 117
moral, 128
mutiny, 123
myth, 13

navigate, 96
negative, 123
nestle, 96
neutral, 103
nomad, 45
numerous, 19

observant, 63
obstacle, 25
overwhelm, 31

peer, 135
persecute, 45
pitiless, 103
plea, 97
poll, 85
portable, 91
postpone, 25
presentable, 103
preserve, 117
prey, 91
primary, 63
principle, 97
productive, 19
provoke, 51
pursue, 123

realistic, 97
reign, 123
reject, 13
rejoice, 57
reliable, 57
resign, 63
rigid, 135
rotate, 103
rowdy, 135

safeguard, 135
sanitary, 117
scorch, 129
scuffle, 13
security, 97
selective, 97

senseless, 57
severe, 129
shred, 103
shrewd, 19
shrivel, 57
singular, 123
solitary, 13
soothe, 85
span, 31
spectacle, 129
sprawl, 117
spurt, 51
straggle, 25
strategy, 19
strive, 63
supreme, 45
swindle, 123

tart, 97
temporary, 13
thrifty, 91
tragic, 129
transport, 45
treacherous, 25
trespass, 135
trifle, 129

undoing, 51
universal, 129

vast, 51
verdict, 63
veteran, 13
vicinity, 85
villain, 19
visual, 91
vivid, 25

widespread, 117
withdraw, 51